WHO WILL BUY THIS?

A VALUER'S PERSPECTIVE ON RISK, EXIT, AND LENDING VALUATION

NIKHIL SINGH JAMWAL

Made with ♥ on the Notion Press Platform
www.notionpress.com

Contents

Preface .... *v*

A Note from the Author .... *vii*

PART: 1

1. The Mistake Out Of Laziness 3
2. Technology Is An Illusion In Rural India 6
3. Real-Time Due Diligence Linked With Sutta 9
4. One Room, Two Loans 12
5. LTV Cushion And Business Call 15
6. Plotting With High Marketability But With No Roads 17
7. When One Village Became The Portfolio 21
8. When The Profile Was Stronger Than The Property 25
9. The Most Dangerous Sentence In Valuation 30
10. The Loan That Looked Small But Behaved Big 33
11. When Competition Replaced Conviction 36
12. Why Conservative Valuations Never Get Credit 39
13. Why Valuers Eventually Become Salesmen 43
14. The Problem Of OTC Conditions In Valuations 47
15. When Right Decision Has No Rulebook 51
16. Valuation — Not A Support Function 54

PART: 2

17. The Psychology Of Property Buyers 59
18. Balance Transfer — The Illusion Of Safety 66
19. The Ecosystem Nobody Mentions In The Sanction Letter 71
20. When Collateral Went Digital — But The Map Is Still Catching Up 74
21. What Valuation Really Teaches You About India 77

Contents

22. The Street Is The Final Teacher 82

23. The Quiet Role Of Women In Mortgage Discipline 84

24. The Hidden National Network Of Valuers In Nation Building 90

25. Why Valuers Often Make The Best Collection Officers In Housing Finance 96

26. The Civil Engineer's Natural Profession 101

27. Why Valuers Rarely Become CEOs 103

28. The New Generation And The Old Boardroom 108

29. A Changing Mortgage Landscape 113

30. The Future Of Leadership In Housing Finance 115

31. The Digital Future Of Collateral — Where Valuation Is Heading 116

Closing Note 123

Appendix — Glossary & Acronyms 125

Preface

Property valuation is often seen as a technical exercise—measuring land, calculating costs, comparing transactions, and producing a number that financial institutions can rely on. But anyone who has spent enough time in the field knows that valuation is rarely just about numbers.

Over the years, walking through countless streets, inspecting houses, and observing neighborhoods across the country, I began to realize that every valuation assignment reveals something deeper about how India works. A property is never just a structure. It is part of a living ecosystem shaped by families, local economies, infrastructure, regulations, and sometimes by informal systems that grow faster than official records.

Working in valuation places one in a unique position. You stand between the formal world of finance and the everyday realities of the street. Banks see collateral. Families see their home. The valuer must understand both.

This book is a collection of reflections from that intersection.

It explores the many lessons that emerge from the mortgage ecosystem—lessons about collateral, borrower behavior, institutional pressures, digitization of land records, and the quiet economics of neighborhoods that ultimately determine the real value of property.

These are not textbook explanations of valuation techniques. Instead, they are observations from the field—lessons that only become visible when you spend enough time looking at property markets, not just through reports, but through the streets where those properties stand.

In many ways, valuation becomes a lens through which one can observe a country constantly building itself—one house, one street, and one neighborhood at a time.

To reflect the journey, the book is divided into two parts:

PART 1: It brings together stories from the ground—real situations, unusual cases, professional dilemmas, and practical lessons from the field. These chapters focus on the realities that professionals encounter when theory meets the street.

PART 2: Itmoves beyond individual cases to examine the deeper forces that shape value: buyer psychology, digitization, leadership, market evolution, challenges in the collateral landscape, and the future of valuation in a rapidly transforming world.

At its core, valuation is not only about property. It is about people, incentives, trust, aspiration, risk, and change. If read carefully, valuation becomes a lens through which one can observe a nation building itself—one home, one street, one neighborhood at a time.

I hope these reflections speak not only to valuers but to everyone interested in finance, housing, markets, and the hidden systems that shape everyday life.

A Note From The Author

To say that writing this book has been an enriching experience would perhaps be an understatement. **"Who Will Buy This? — A Valuer's Perspective on Risk, Exit, and Lending Valuation"** grew slowly out of years spent walking through neighborhoods, inspecting homes, speaking to borrowers, and observing how property markets quietly shape the financial ecosystem of the country.

For most people, valuation is a technical activity—measurements, documentation, reports, and numbers. But those who spend enough time in the field soon realize that the profession is far more than that. Behind every property lies a story: of families building homes, of neighborhoods evolving, of institutions managing risk, and of a country constantly transforming itself through the simple act of people creating places to live.

This book is an attempt to capture some of those observations.

Over the years, my work in housing finance and property valuation has allowed me to see India from a perspective that few professions experience so closely. A ***valuer*** walks through streets that rarely appear in policy discussions, meets people whose financial decisions quietly sustain the mortgage system, and observes how markets behave long before the numbers appear in reports.

The lessons in this book come from that world—the world behind the ***valuation report.***

They are reflections on *collateral*, lending behavior, institutional pressures, digitization of land records, and the human realities that influence how property markets function in India. Many of these lessons were not learned in classrooms or policy documents. They were learned while standing in front of houses, speaking to neighbors, reading the character of a street, and trying to understand how value truly emerges in the real world.

Along this journey, I have been fortunate to work with many talented professionals whose contributions quietly shape the housing finance ecosystem. I would like to extend my sincere gratitude to all the technical managers and valuation professionals I have worked with over the years. Their experience, judgement, and practical wisdom from the field have been invaluable in shaping many of the insights reflected in this book.

A special word of appreciation also goes to the ground teams and field staff who spend long hours traveling across towns, villages, and expanding city fringes to verify properties, interact with communities, and bring the realities of the market back into the system. Much of what we understand about property markets comes from these countless site visits, conversations, and observations made on the ground.

Every field visit teaches something new, and many of the reflections in this book are the result of those experiences—the long days on the road, the inspections across unfamiliar streets, and the many conversations that reveal how markets function beyond reports and policies.

Finally, I would like to thank the reader for taking the time to explore these observations. If this book helps professionals see the profession of valuation a little differently—not only as a technical task but as a lens through which one can observe how markets and communities evolve—then it will have served its purpose.

Because in the end, valuation teaches one quiet but powerful lesson: The reports may contain numbers, but the real story of value is always waiting outside—on the street.

A glossary of terms used in this book is provided at the end for reference.

PART: 1

CHAPTER 1

The Mistake Out of Laziness

I still remember the scorching heat of Delhi in the month of July 2013. I was out on my shared Hero Splendor, searching for an address far away from the place where I used to live. Natively from Jammu, I studied in Pune and have now moved across four different cities in the country. I never realized that one day I would be riding a motorcycle, trying to find my way through roads I had never thought I would land on.

That's how my journey of valuation started.

The property I was visiting that day was a small house in the rural fringe of a tier-3 town, away from the city bustle, with no proper address to locate it. The only thing I had to rely on was trust, and perhaps the digital maps made available to us (thanks to the Ambanis for making data accessible across the country).

All I had with me was my diary, a measuring tape, my company identity card, and a helmet (of course).

After reaching the site (guided by the customer), two things struck me: First, I had no reliable way to independently verify whether the property shown to me was the same property mentioned in the documents. There was no proper address, no strong digital mapping support, and no easy method of cross-checking location details in real time. I was depending largely on the borrower's guidance. What if it was all a setup? What tools did I really have at that time to cross-verify?

Second, I realized how limited a valuer's tools were in those days. Beyond physical inspection, local enquiry, and personal judgement, there was very little data available to test assumptions or detect misrepresentation. If the case had been structured to mislead, uncovering it would have been extremely difficult.

I continued with the process, measured the site, took a selfie (yes, it's been part of the process for a long time), asked for the valuation of the property from the customer himself, noted down the details in the diary, and fled like a hungry man who had been waiting to eat for years.

Six months later, I was asked to revisit the same property. By then, the loan had turned delinquent, and recovery action had begun under SARFAESI.

This time, the borrower raised a serious objection. He claimed that the property shown during the original valuation was not the asset actually intended to be mortgaged. According to him, the lender had taken security over a different property than the one he believed was being offered.

In simple terms, the identity of the collateral itself had come under dispute.

For those who may not know, SARFAESI is the legal framework under which lenders enforce security in case of default.

That was the first incident that had taught me the importance of the job I was doing. I couldn't sleep that night. The curious mind kept asking: What could have gone wrong? What did I miss? How could I have prevented it?

I realized I could have done more. I should have spoken to the neighbors. I should have enquired beyond what was presented to me. I had relied too much on what the borrower showed and ignored the basics of independent verification.

After days of thinking about it, one thing became very clear to me. "It was a mistake out of laziness."

Lesson 1#

In valuations, trust is earned through documents and enquiries, not through processes alone.

Recommendations from the chapter

1. The trick to valuing unregulated real estate in India, especially where there are no municipal or ward numbers, lies in enquiries and on-ground intelligence, not just assessing the asset in isolation.
2. Listen to the customer, but do not accept everything at face value. As they say, there are many good actors around, and sometimes your customer might just be one of them.
3. Question every assumption, especially in small-ticket housing.
4. Always match documents with the physical building and measure the property, even if it is raining, remote, or inconvenient.
5. Treat the money as your own. Once that mindset is in place, the right decisions tend to follow.

CHAPTER 2

Technology Is an Illusion in Rural India

One of my company's smartest engineers, posted in a small town in Madhya Pradesh, once decided to conduct a site visit without informing the branch.

That day, he wanted to challenge rural India. But rural India, as always, had its own way of challenging back.

In India, just like every city seems to have an "MG Road", many villages across districts share the same name.

What looks simple on a map rarely behaves that way on the ground.

He called the borrower and asked for the location on WhatsApp.

"Sir, bas Google location pe aa jaiye. Seedha ghar par hi pahunch jaoge." (Sir, just arrive at the Google location. You will reach the house.)

Confident about the technology, he followed the map.

A few minutes later, he found himself standing in the middle of an open field.

Flowers were swaying in the wind.

Google Maps calmly announced, "You have arrived at your destination."

There was no house. No boundary. No road. Just a cow grazing peacefully, looking at him as if asking, "Batao, kya dhoond rahe ho?" (Tell me what you are looking for.)

Confused, he called the borrower. "Sir, I am here. Where is your house?"

The borrower replied casually, "Arre, woh doosra gaon hai. Aap galat gaon mein chale gaye." (That's another village. You have reached the wrong village.)

That day, he learned something Google never teaches.

In many parts of India, within every 30–50 kilometers, you will find villages with identical names. For a valuer, this changes everything.

Valuation is not about reaching a location. It is about identifying the correct location.

And that identification cannot be outsourced to an app.

In this case, the engineer made two mistakes:

First, he did not thoroughly verify the sale deed and property details before starting the visit.

Second, he blindly trusted technology.

Both mistakes are common. And both are dangerous.

Lesson 2#

In valuations, technology can guide you to a location, but only documents and on-ground intelligence can confirm you are at the right one.

Recommendations from the chapter

1. A valuer's job is not just to reach the location shared by the customer. It is to analyse and establish the identity of the property through documents.
2. Always match key attributes from the documents, such as property area (as per site vs. as per records), boundaries, and revenue details.
3. Landmarks matter more than pins. Benchmark distances from known identifiers—an Anganwadi, school, chowk, temple—anything that locals recognize.
4. Location risk is real collateral risk. If the property itself is not correctly identified, everything else in the valuation becomes irrelevant.

CHAPTER 3

Real-Time Due Diligence Linked with Sutta

It was peak summer—the kind where your phone overheats before your brain does. One of my team members was on an assignment in a small village near Indore. The loan amount applied was ₹10 lakhs, and the document available for cross-verification reflected open land instead of a house.

GPS in the rural fringes of India is still a challenge. Those who say it's not have probably never been on the ground.

Dodging cows, kids, and a couple of friendly dogs, he reached the spot where the borrower had guided him. He tried contacting the borrower, who shared someone else's number—a person named Shekhawat.

Shekhawat replied, "Saab, main toh bahar hoon, aap road ke dusri taraf tapri pe aa jao. Tab tak chai pi lijiye." (Sir, I am out. You wait at the tea stall on the other side of the road. Have some tea till then.)

And that's how it started—his most unusual, yet most revealing site visit.

He ordered one cup of tea and a cigarette—cigarette only to stretch the conversation, because tea finishes faster.

While taking a puff, he casually asked the chaiwala, "Yahan Rinku Singh ka ghar kahan hai?" (Where is Rinku Singh's home?)

The chaiwala replied, "Rinku Singh toh kab ke guzar gaye." (Rinku Singh passed away a long time ago.)

He asked further, "Toh unke ghar pe kaun rehta hai?" (Who lives in his home now?)

The chaiwala said, "Saab, woh ghar toh kaafi saalon se khaali pada hai. Sab shehar shift ho gaye." (Sir, the house has been vacant for years. They've all moved to the city.)

He lit another cigarette. This time, his brain had started moving faster; he knew something was off.

He called the person who was supposed to show the property. After some time, the person arrived and took him to the site.

The house was dilapidated, exactly as described by the chaiwala.

Shekhawat was in a hurry. He avoided answering questions, insisted that no photos be taken, and clearly didn't want the valuer speaking to neighbors. The intent was obvious—keep everything within a controlled narrative.

My team member started matching the property details in the documents with what he saw on-site. Nothing matched.

He was now certain that this was an attempt to misrepresent the entire case.

As he was about to leave, he asked one last question. "Where is Rinku Singh, and what is your relation with him?"

Shekhawat replied, "Rinku bhai khet pe gaye hain. Main unka chhota bhai hoon. Hum isi ghar mein rehte hain." (Rinku has gone to the fields. I am his younger brother, and we live here.)

The contradiction was complete.

That day, my team member prevented a potential fraud of ₹10 lakhs, all because a conversation started with what we casually label as "injurious to health."

Lesson 3#

In valuations, truth does not sit in the file. It walks around the plot, sits by the wall, and sometimes waits patiently at the chai tapri.

(Non-smokers can manage with a few extra cups of tea.)

Recommendations from the chapter

1. In smaller locations, borrower transparency improves when you blend in, not when you arrive with authority.
2. Local chaiwalas, shopkeepers, and neighbors often provide stronger risk signals than formal data sources.

That chai tapri is your conference room. The tea glass is your due diligence form. And the people around you are your real risk indicators.

CHAPTER 4

One Room, Two Loans

Soon after Ajay finished his visits for the day, one assignment under the name of Bal Krishan was still pending. It had been a hectic day, and he initially thought of pushing the visit to the next day.

However, when he checked his diary, he noticed that the location of the last case was close to where he was.

He put on his helmet, kicked his motorcycle with his already tired legs, and headed towards what would be his final visit of the day.

One thing that triggered him to visit the property was the customer's continuous calls. Something felt unusual.

Customers usually don't call repeatedly for a visit, but this one kept insisting: "Sir, aap aa jaiye. Engineer Sahab... chai ban raha hai." (Sir, please come. Engineer Sir... tea is being prepared.)

This was both intriguing and slightly unusual.

On his way, he called the branch and asked for the complete set of documents. Out of curiosity, he read them thoroughly before reaching the site to understand the basics of the case.

He reached the site, and the customers came out and started behaving as if they had known him for years.

He began measuring the property and completing the formalities as per the process.

There was one room and a kitchen that remained locked.

Every time he asked about it, the customer casually avoided the question, saying: "Yeh mehmaan ke liye hai." (This is for guests.)

Surprisingly, that was the only portion that did not match the registry documents.

At that moment, he understood that the customer was deliberately trying to include that portion to increase the loan amount and valuation.

He didn't confront the customer immediately.

Instead, he quietly observed the entire property and left.

He then reached out to his network—financiers and contacts active in that area.

After a few calls, he discovered that the extra portion had already been mortgaged with another housing finance company.

He immediately flagged the case. The customer and the sourcing agent were subsequently blacklisted.

Lesson 4#

In valuations, when a customer is overly friendly even before the visit, your inner "Sherlock Holmes" should stay alert. Not everyone who offers chai is waiting to serve you.

Recommendations from the chapter

1. Awareness during site visits is critical. Finishing within *TAT* is important, but an alert and strategic approach helps prevent such fraud.
2. Your network in the industry, especially with other valuers and financiers, is a strong asset. Use it.
3. The devil is always in the details. Preparation before the visit helps you connect the dots better. Read documents carefully and understand the case before stepping on-site.
4. Never let your curiosity switch off. A valuer must stay curious about the ***micro-market***, location dynamics, proximity to key areas, physical and social infrastructure, and legal aspects. Curiosity helps uncover small but critical facts that protect the mortgage.

CHAPTER 5

LTV Cushion and Business Call

It was a routine field visit to a compact row house colony on the outskirts of Jalgaon. The borrower had applied for a loan amount of ₹ 20 lakhs. One of my team members had visited the property and found many anomalies in the locality, starting from the access road to transactions in the micro market.

It was a small village with a population of barely 1,000 people, and no established infrastructure. Out of his curiosity, the valuer randomly started asking the local villagers about the recent transactions.

The response was simple: "This is a small village where everyone knows each other, most are related, and there have been hardly any sale-purchase transactions. Houses are generally constructed on agricultural land and passed down within families."

This discussion raised concerns for the valuer. Many questions started running through his mind:

- Is it even correct to call this lending secured?
- What reasons should be given to reject such a case upfront?

He gathered his courage and proposed the case to his seniors. As expected, the response was to consider an *LTV* cushion. The LTV was fixed at 50%, and he was forced to release the report treating LTV as a mitigating factor.

After one year, the same case turned delinquent. Even at 50% LTV, the HFC was unable to liquidate the asset, as no transactions were possible in that particular area. Exactly as highlighted during the valuation.

Lesson 5#

In valuations, the LTV cushion is a myth. A non-marketable collateral will remain non-marketable, even if the LTV is low.

Recommendations from the chapter

1. Always rely on ground-level real estate enquiries. Do not treat LTV as a justification to proceed with a weak case.
2. Outstanding dues and legal charges increase rapidly during enforcement. A non-marketable collateral will remain unsold, irrespective of how conservative the LTV appears.

Credit teams should share LTV expectations with valuers. Valuation must remain independent and should not be influenced by the intended loan structure.

CHAPTER 6

Plotting with High Marketability but with No Roads

India's housing finance, especially the affordable housing segment, is gaining a lot of attention from foreign investors. With promoters diluting their equity, pressure mounts significantly on increasing valuations by accelerating growth and aggressively growing Assets Under Management.

This same pressure flows down to branches, and in the race to achieve targets, most of us tend to forget the basics of mortgage valuation.

In this highly profitable business of secured lending, what makes the product secured is the collateral, and when we don't take it seriously, the portfolio is bound to take a hit in the long run.

As we move towards extended municipal limits, collaterals often lack proper legal documentation and requisite approvals, unlike approved colonies. There are many small landowners who hold inherited agricultural land in acres and benefit from rising land prices due to urbanization moving outward. Many small villages across India are going through this transition. Every such landowner eventually becomes a "plotter", as they say.

Those who own land near a road start carving out plots from large land parcels and sell them to investors. Investors buy these plots expecting future urbanization and appreciation in land prices.

However, such plotting:

- lacks proper infrastructure
- lacks a social ecosystem
- and most importantly, remains unapproved

Even identification is weak, with temporary numbering being assigned to plots instead of formal records.

There are two ways to look at this. First: Why is the government not stopping such unapproved plotting? Second: What kind of borrowers are investing in such plots where even basic infrastructure is not available?

To answer the first: The development of such plotting carries both political and economic angles.

These plots are typically available at prices much lower than approved colonies—sometimes even 4–5 times cheaper. This segment caters to a large base of affordable buyers, which also aligns with a significant voter base.

Hence, enforcement is limited, and the perceived risk of demolition or strict action remains low in many such areas.

Secondly, the buyer profile is equally important.

Many buyers:

- belong to nearby villages
- have moved out for work
- and want to own a property close to their native place

This emotional and practical combination drives demand in such plotting.

Many valuers working with housing finance companies encounter such cases regularly.

The major challenges in such properties include:

- identification issues
- lack of clear access roads
- absence of formal layout
- and difficulty in validating ***comparables***

One very common condition observed is: "Marking of the road shall be done before ***disbursement.***"

Trust me, in most cases, this is only to ensure that the file moves forward and targets are met. This road is not meant to be properly developed. The "developer" is often just a landowner whose family has owned the land for years and is now selling parts of it.

Lesson 6#

In mortgage valuation, a property may look sellable on paper, but without proper physical access, legal clarity, and usable infrastructure, marketability remains incomplete.

Recommendations from the chapter

1. As a valuer, there is a need to shift the mindset of the system from customer-centric to collateral-centric, especially in secured lending.
2. For such plotting cases, a separate SOP should be created, clearly defining:
   - do's and don'ts
   - additional documents required
   - risk indicators specific to such layouts
3. LTV in such cases should be linked to the realizable value of the property in a distress or auction scenario—not just the perceived market value.
4. Use of cadastral maps and geo-informatics systems to superimpose village maps on site coordinates should be encouraged and gradually made *standard practice.* Training of valuers should also align with this.

CHAPTER 7

When One Village Became the Portfolio

It did not begin with a strategy; it began with success. A small cluster of lower-middle-income borrowers, self-constructed homes, repayment discipline, and community stability.

The first few files performed beautifully. EMIs were regular. Collections were smooth. Recovery calls were rare. The branch felt confident.

- "This belt is strong."
- "People here don't default."
- "Community pressure works."

And so the files increased.

Concentration rarely feels like risk at the beginning. It feels like efficiency.

The valuer knows the lanes. The branch knows the households. The micro-market feels predictable. Travel time reduces. Assessment becomes faster, but discussions get shorter. In lower-middle-income segments, social cohesion is often seen as security.

Borrowers live close. Families know each other. Reputation matters. There is pride in repayment. But concentration does not care about pride. It cares about correlation. If twenty homes sit within walking distance of each other, they may look independent on paper, but economically, they are not, and they usually share the same employment ecosystem, the same local contractor base, the same access roads, the same informal land history, and the same political climate. They rise together and struggle together. The portfolio view hides this reality. In MIS, the files look separate.

Different borrowers. Different loan numbers. Different sanction dates. But the exit buyer does not see the loan numbers. The exit buyer sees geography, and when stress hits one geography, ***liquidity*** dries up for all. It does not take a disaster; it takes a shift.

There was a time when we reviewed a cluster where over 68% of the branch's books sat within a few kilometers. On paper, performance was healthy. But during a stress simulation, one uncomfortable question surfaced: "If we had to auction ten assets here within six months, who would buy them?"

Silence followed.

Because the answer was clear: the same small buyer base that had originally absorbed them. Market depth was an illusion.

Lower-middle-income housing behaves differently. Buyers are often: Agriculture dependent, informal salary dependent, and emotionally attached. When stress comes, external villagers hesitate. Liquidity depends on local circulation, not institutional absorption. It is not a fraud; it is structural fragility.

Branches and Risk

Early warning signals are rarely noticed this early. Even if they do, who would have the courage to stop the running business?

Housing finance often speaks about ticket size. "Small loan, small risk."

But concentration converts small risks into systematic ones. Because when stress hits a cluster, social narratives amplify, and liquidity becomes competitive within the same portfolio.

The irony is this: The branch that performs best initially is often the one that accumulates the highest concentration.

Success creates replication. Replication creates clustering. Clustering creates hidden correlation. And correlation only reveals itself during stress.

Valuation must think beyond file-level safety. It must ask:

- What percentage of this branch's books sit within a 5-kilometer radius?
- How many loans depend on one resale corridor?
- How many customers rely on the same income cluster?

Because diversification is not a credit metric alone, it is a valuation responsibility. A village is not risky because it is rural; a cluster is risky because it is concentrated, and concentration hides inside performance.

Lesson 7#

A strong cluster can create confidence, but overconcentration quietly creates risk. What looks efficient in growth can become fragile in stress.

Recommendations from the chapter

1. Introduce micro-geography gaps. Set internal exposure thresholds at the village or ward level, not just the district level.
2. Track radius-based exposure. Measure the percentage of the portfolio within 1-kilometer, 3-kilometer, and 5-kilometer clusters.
3. Conduct liquidity stress tests. Periodically simulate simultaneous auctions within a cluster and assess buyer absorption capacity.
4. Map economic correlation. Identify clusters dependent on the same employer, contractor ecosystem, or the same channel.

CHAPTER 8

When the Profile Was Stronger than the Property

The file was impressive.

Government salaried employee, twenty years of service, stable salary credits, clean bureau history, and existing home loan closed successfully. The branch was confident before the site visit even happened.

"This is a clean green channel profile case." That phrase carries comfort.

A clean green channel profile means: Income is strong. EMI capacity is high. The bureau is clean. Risk appears borrower-centric, not asset-centric. Next comes the collateral ***underwriting***.

The property, in this case, was a self-constructed house in a rapidly expanding settlement. Narrow roads, informal drainage, mixed construction quality around, and limited resale evidence and secondary market.

The valuation team flagged a soft caution, suggesting, "The market depth appears to be limited beyond buyers, hence ***marketability*** is average."

Credit responded calmly, "Even if the asset is slow to move, the borrower capacity is strong."

The distinction was subtle; the conversation had shifted. From asset safety to borrower strength. This is how profile funding quietly begins influencing valuation posture.

When a profile is strong, three silent shifts occur:

- LTV stretch feels comfortable.
- Liquidity concerns are softened.
- Asset quality scrutiny becomes proportional to borrower risk.

But valuation discipline should never be proportional to borrower comfort, because borrower strength and asset strength are separate risk variables. They intersect only when a default occurs, and a default does not seek permission from income stability.

Months later, the same customer relocated for a new posting, and the property was put on sale. Not on stress, not under distress, just a life change. The branch informally tried to assess the market response.

Enquiries were limited. Negotiations were steep, time extended; the asset was not defective, but it was just illiquid. A strong profile had masked a weak exit depth.

In mortgages, a strong profile influences the valuation more in subtle ways. When Credit believes the borrower is solid, the valuation commentary feels like friction.

The question becomes: "Why are we overanalyzing collateral for such a clean case?"

But most of the time, this question misunderstands the role of collateral. Collateral is not there to support good borrowers; it is there to protect capital when good borrowers face unpredictable events, and unpredictability is the only constant in the long-tenure lending.

In lower middle-income segments, profile strength is often employment-based. Government Job. First salary but stable tenure. But assets may still sit in: Thin resale corridors, informal layouts, narrow access lanes, and limited buyer depth pockets.

When valuation begins calibrating its caution based on profile quality, independence erodes silently.

There is also a psychological bias. Strong profiles create institutional confidence. What I have experienced is that confidence reduces resistance, and resistance is necessary in valuation.

Not emotional resistance, analytical resistance. The discipline to say, "The borrower is excellent, but the asset is average," is rare.

Funding based on only the profile also affects portfolio behavior. High-income borrowers often pre-pay faster, which creates shorter average tenure. When valuation over-relaxes on such cases, the illusion is: "Even if risk exists, exposure duration is low."

But prepayment behavior is unpredictable.

Interest rate shifts, market movements, and employment changes. Assumptions about early closure cannot replace asset integrity. There is a bigger institutional risk. If valuation standards become softer for strong profiles, the portfolio gradually accumulates asset inconsistency. On paper, borrower risk looks diversified. In reality, asset quality varies silently. That variation only surfaces when an asset needs to exit, and exit does not ask about bureau score; it asks for the buyer's depth.

I have often heard these dangerous statements from senior business and credit leaders: "This is more of a profile case." Because of this sentence, collateral is time and again being redefined as a secondary comfort.

Profile reduces the probability of default, but collateral reduces the severity of loss; both are independent safeguards. Weakening one because of the other causes a structural imbalance.

Years later, during a portfolio stress review, we noticed something subtle. It was highest in strong profile cases where asset quality had been assumed acceptable. When a rare default happened, the exit depth was poor. Confidence had replaced caution.

Onboarding quality profiles is not a problem, but adjusting the valuation methodologies based on the profile is.

The discipline lies in separating: Borrower, confidence, asset liquidity, and loan-sizing logic; each must stand independently. If one influences the other too much, objectivity fades.

Lesson 8#

A strong borrower can repay the loan, but only a strong asset can secure it. In secured lending, profile strength should never replace collateral discipline.

Recommendations from the chapter

1. Separate borrower strength from asset valuation. Valuation notes must not dilute collateral commentary based on income quality. Managements should start democratized and prioritize valuation opinion.
2. Standardize asset security across profiles. Institutionalize the location risk as standard for country, marketability, and buyer depth should be the decider for onboarding, same location risk must carry the same caution irrespective of the borrower segment.
3. Cap LTV based on liquidity, not income. Most of the offered LTV programmes in the mortgage business choose parameters of income as a standard and avoid the location-centric approach; the loan sizing discipline must prioritize exit depth over EMI comfort.
4. Reinforce collateral philosophy internally.Institutional messaging must emphasize asset truth independent of borrower strength.

CHAPTER 9

The Most Dangerous Sentence in Valuation

The sentence didn't arrive with authority. It arrived casually, almost kindly.

"This is standard practice."

It was said across a table, between sips of tea, in a room where everyone wanted the file to move.

No one challenged it. No one needed to. The sentence had already done its work.

Valuation practice never begins as a standard. It begins as a workaround. A temporary adjustment. A one-time exception that worked.

Then it works again, and again, and again. Soon, no one remembers why it was introduced. Only that it exists.

"Why do we do such cases?" someone asks.

"This," comes the reply, "is a standard practice."

The sentence feels safe because it spreads responsibility. If everyone does it, no one owns it. If no one owns it, no one is accountable.

The valuer defends its judgement and starts borrowing the system's comfort. His reports still look professional, his tone still remains cautious, but his attitude has been outsourced.

Standard practice becomes a shield—thin, but comforting.

There was a time when asking why felt natural.
Now it feels disruptive. The valuer hesitates.

He doesn't want to look inexperienced.
He doesn't want to slow things down.
He doesn't want to be the only one uncomfortable when everyone seems comfortable.

So he accepts the explanation.

He nods.
He moves on.

This is not a compromise.
This is surrender disguised as maturity.

Years later, the same file returns, this time from recovery.

The property is up for auction.
The reserve price is correct.
The documents are still clean.

And yet, no one shows.

The market doesn't recognize standard practice. It recognizes only desire, access, and confidence.

Lesson 9#

The phrase "standard practice" is not a substitute for logic, policy, or accountability. Repeated mistakes do not become acceptable merely because they are common.

Recommendations from the chapter

1. Markets do not reward standard operating procedures; they reward strong judgement. One lesson that has stayed with me from field operations to boardroom is this: The right decisions can be unpopular in the moment, yet invaluable later. When a loan defaults, no one debates the elegance of the process. The market only asks a simpler question: Was the asset underwritten well? In the end, recovery does not applaud procedure. It validates prudence.
2. Rotate valuers across familiar micro-markets. Repetition breeds blind acceptance; rotation restores skepticism. An early warning indicator is the best indicator for any location to stay up to date.
3. Treat "standard practice" as a trigger, not an answer. Whenever this phrase appears, it should prompt deeper scrutiny, not closure.
4. Reward questioning, not just TAT. In today's financial ecosystem, rewarding TAT becomes a hobby. Valuers boast of reducing TAT, which results in massive leakage of valuations and no control in the future. If institutions start promoting the culture of questioning and not just reducing TAT, this will help the institutions in a big way.

CHAPTER 10

The Loan That Looked Small but Behaved Big

The loan amount was ₹8.3 lakhs, and that itself made everyone comfortable. It was a small-ticket, affordable housing case for a first-time borrower—the kind of file institutions often consider routine and low-risk.

In many lending environments, the label "affordable housing" can unintentionally lower the intensity of scrutiny. The case appears simple, modest, and familiar. Nothing about it seems alarming.

I still remember someone in the office calling it the "bread and butter" segment.

Sixteen months later, the EMI stopped coming. Not all at once, but in stages. There was an initial delay, followed by restructuring requests, and then complete silence. By the time the account slipped into NPA, the outstanding amount remained small, but the effort required to manage it had grown disproportionately.

Small-ticket defaults are often expensive to resolve. Field visits, legal notices, repeated follow-ups, local resistance, and borrower counselling consume time and resources. In this case, the cost of attention had already begun to exceed the size of the loan.

The real challenge emerged when recovery reached the collateral. The property existed, the borrower had surrendered, and the original valuation was within a reasonable range. Yet there was no buyer interest.

The village was small, socially concentrated, and largely inactive from a resale perspective. There were few comparable transactions and little visible economic momentum. Auction notices were issued more than once, but no bidders came forward.

That modest loan, once treated as routine business, had become a management issue. Weak underwriting choices, ignored early warning signals, and poor marketability had quietly turned a small exposure into a large operational burden.

The loss was not only financial. It was managerial and structural.

Small loans rarely fail dramatically. More often, they drain institutions slowly, and portfolios suffer through the accumulation of many such cases.

Affordable housing may be built on empathy, but housing finance must also be built on recoverability. A lower ticket size can create comfort, but it does not reduce legal complexity, shorten liquidation timelines, or create a secondary market where none exists.

A ₹1 crore property in a strong municipal market may still attract buyers at a distressed price. A ₹10 lakh property in an illiquid location often attracts only questions, and unanswered questions can stall recovery for years.

Risk in housing finance does not always rise in proportion to ticket size. In many cases, a small loan on a weak asset can be more dangerous than a large loan on a strong one, because recovery costs do not shrink with the loan amount.

Most institutions track disbursement growth, ticket size, and collection efficiency. Far fewer track effort per default, cost per recovery, or management attention consumed per rupee lent. That is why some small loans appear safe—until they are tested.

Lesson 10#

A small loan is not always a small risk. In affordable housing, modest ticket sizes can hide huge servicing costs, recovery complexity, and disproportionate portfolio stress.

Recommendations from the chapter

1. Stop equating small ticket size with low risk. For a valuer, an asset valuation parameter should not differ when loans are small. Affordable housing loans must be assessed for exit complexity, not emotional comfort.
2. Avoid sympathy-led valuations. Borrower intention does not reduce asset friction in the future.

Trust the decision your valuer is making. Institutions need to trust their valuers' remarks and should consider them as a final decision engine. Recovery comes from assets, and if the valuer who has valued that asset is not comfortable, we are not building an institution; we are waiting for disaster to happen.

CHAPTER 11

When Competition Replaced Conviction

The first time it happened, no one noticed. That's usually how it begins.

The valuer was packing up after a long day when his phone rang.

"Can you recheck one thing?" the sales manager asked. "Your value looks conservative."

The valuer opened the report again. Same identity, same asset, same assumptions, nothing has changed since morning.

"Conservative compared to what?" the valuer asked.

There was a pause. "Compared to what the competition is giving."

The next day, the file came back, this time with numbers.

Three lenders. Three values. All higher.

No explanation of why those values existed. Just the fact that they did.

The unspoken question hung in the air: Are we missing something, or are we just slow?

The valuer revisited the site. Nothing had changed. The access road was still narrow. The market was still thin. The secondary market was similar. But now doubt had entered, not about the property, but about himself.

If everyone else is comfortable, why am I not? Am I overthinking the risk?

He didn't increase the value drastically; that would have felt wrong. He adjusted the tone. The same concern was now described as manageable. The same limitation became common in the locality. The same risk was contextualized. The numbers moved slightly, but not enough to stand out.

The file moved on. No further questions. No follow-ups. No justification needed. The relief was immediate. Being aligned felt professional; being different had felt tiring.

Over the next few months, it happened again, and again, not with the instructions, not with pressure, but because a precedent of the value had been duly set in the valuer's mind.

The institution still claimed a strong valuation philosophy, but philosophy is not what you say; it is what you defend when it becomes inconvenient.

Three years later, the same property appeared, but in recovery discussions. The sales manager had left, the valuer had left, and an entirely new team had arrived. The valuer had given a 40% discount on the current value and claimed that this was the correct value. All of a sudden, that call, which was an exception to meet the competition expectation, was hovering over the current team and asking for justification.

That's how the concept of overvaluation originates in reality.

Lesson 11#

Valuation should be driven by evidence, not by competitor numbers. The moment market pressure replaces independent conviction, risk enters disguised as growth.

Recommendations from the chapter

1. Do not benchmark valuation outcomes; benchmark losses. Peer comparison should happen at recovery and NPA reviews, not at sanction. Valuations that align today often fail together later.
2. Separate the market noise with market depth. Multiple lenders funding the same asset does not create liquidity. Valuation must assess who will buy in distress, not who has funded.
3. Audit files where values were revised after comparison. These files carry higher systemic risk and should be reviewed periodically. Hindsight should be a process.
4. Management plays a role in creating a differentiator.Collateral-led management always looks up to its valuers. That is the key to a healthy portfolio. Institutions should reward valuers for extrapolating such risks and not for always being aligned with market forces.

CHAPTER 12

Why Conservative Valuations Never Get Credit

The deal was lost on Saturday. No escalation. No drama. Just a short update in the internal tracker: "Customer not interested, as he got the loan from some other lender." The file was closed.

The property was ordinary. A self-occupied house in a semi-developed pocket. Documents were in place. The borrower profile was stable. The kind of case that usually moves without any friction. But the valuer didn't rush it.

He noticed the access road narrowing near the end of the lane. Saw that demand depended heavily on local familiarity. He checked recent transactions and realized that most of the sales were within the single community and were distress-driven.

He didn't cut the value aggressively. He didn't reject the case. He simply refused to be optimistic and gave a discount in the valuation, which pertained to the transactional discount.

The remarks were measured:

- Marketability limited beyond the local buyer pool.
- Exit dependent on vacant possession and local acceptance.

The value supported a loan, but not the loan that the branch wanted.

The sales manager called, "Others are comfortable at higher values."

The valuer listened and then explained. Calmly, factually.

No arguments followed, but the energy shifted. The file slowed. Next week, the borrower chose another lender. The branch moved on; the target didn't wait.

Something important happened, quietly. The institution did not book a marginal asset, a locality-dependent exit, or a loan requiring explanation in the future. There was no loss to account for; there was no gain to celebrate.

Why does conservative valuation feel like underperformance?

Because it interferes with the momentum and the ecosystem. In today's competitive housing finance environments, speed is mistaken for efficiency. Anything that slows disbursement feels like resistance.

Conservative valuation does exactly that. It asks:

- Who will buy this?
- How fast?
- Without explanation?

Those questions don't help book loans; they help build predictable portfolios, but predictability doesn't excite monthly reviews.

Institutions often measure:

- Sanctions
- Disbursements
- Conversion ratios

They rarely measure:

- Friction avoided
- Decisions not escalated
- Risks filtered upstream

So conservative valuation appears expensive until you notice how many portfolios it has been saving. Time not spent defending marginal assets is time spent scaling the strong ones.

The valuers know something that most dashboards don't. That saying "no" early simplifies credit, stabilizes policy, and reduces emotional decision-making. But he also knows this won't be rewarded, so conviction becomes a personal discipline, not an institutional incentive. That's why philosophy matters.

Lesson 12#

Conservative valuations may lose today's deal, but they often protect tomorrow's portfolio. In risk management, the decisions that save losses rarely receive applause.

Recommendations from the chapter

1. Redefine the success matrix for valuation. Do not judge valuation by conversion or disbursement speed. Measure it by reduction in escalations, exceptions, forced approvals, and collateral portfolio.
2. Institutionalize the right to slow down. Build a formal space for valuation to delay a file without penalty. Speed should never override selectivity.
3. Align credit appetite with valuation selectivity. If the valuation flags exit weakness and loan sizing, the structure must adjust, not the language of the valuation.
4. Capture friction avoided as an outcome. Document all the cases where conservative valuation prevented prolonged discussions, reworks, or escalations.
5. Train leadership to recognize invisible wins. Senior management should consciously acknowledge decisions that simplify portfolios, even when they reduce volumes.

CHAPTER 13

Why Valuers Eventually Become Salesmen

Abhijeet didn't notice the change at first. He had been a valuer for almost eight years now—long enough to know every lane of the district, every broker's voice, every branch manager's impatience.

He wasn't careless. In fact, he was known as one of the reliable ones—quick, cooperative, "business friendly". That label had started appearing in meetings. On one such afternoon, he sat on his bike outside a half-constructed house on the edge of a semi-urban town. The borrower stood beside him, smiling a little too much, offering water, and trying to ease the process.

"Sir, bas formalities hain... aap jaante hi ho," (Sir, it's just formalities... You already know), the borrower said.

Abhijeet had already valued three properties in the same locality last month. Same road—or rather, the same promise of one. Same builder, same story.

Those files had moved fast. No questions from Credit. No callbacks.

He looked at his phone. Four more cases pending. TAT flashed in his head like a countdown clock.

The first small shortcut. He skipped the backside of the plot. Earlier in his career, he would have walked the entire boundary, even if it meant stepping into thorny bushes or asking uncomfortable questions. Today, he relied on memory. Same dimensions. Same orientation. Same everything.

He took the photos, uploaded the geo-tag, and filled in the market rate almost instinctively.

Nothing felt wrong. And that's what made it different. A neighbor was watching him from across the road. Abhijeet noticed but didn't engage. Earlier, he would have crossed over, asked routine questions, and acted casual. Now, he told himself, "It's the same layout."

As he was about to leave, his phone rang.

"Abhijeet Bhai, last case hai na? Please close today. The customer is chasing me," the branch manager said.

The tone was friendly. No pressure. No instruction.

"Ho jayega," (Will do), Abhijeet replied without thinking.

That sentence used to mean: I will check everything and confirm.

Now it meant: I will make it work.

While packing up, the borrower spoke again, "Sir, chhota loan hai... bas ghar ka sapna hai." (Sir, the loan is small... just a dream of a home.)

Abhijeet paused for a second. Affordable housing had taught him many things, one of them being that risk often hides behind innocence.

But in that moment, the human part of him responded first. He softened the remark. Replaced a warning with a suggestion.

That evening, sitting at a tea stall, he overheard two men talking.

"Us layout ka auction hua tha pichle saal..." (There was an auction of that layout last year.)

"Koi aaya hi nahi." (No one came.)

Abhijeet froze. The words mattered immediately. A failed auction often reveals something that documents do not. It can indicate weak buyer demand, poor location acceptance, title concerns, access issues, or simply a market where transactions are far slower than expected.

On paper, the property could still appear adequate. But valuation is not only about what an asset should be worth; it is also about how easily that value can be realized when needed.

If the market had already rejected the same locality once, then the risk profile of the case was different from what his report reflected.

For the first time that day, Abhijeet realized that a valuer can be technically correct, still commercially wrong.

Lesson 13#

The day a valuer starts valuing speed, relationships, or business convenience above independent judgement, he stops protecting collateral and starts behaving like sales.

Recommendations from the chapter

1. Never measure performance only by TAT. A fast report is not always a good report. Institutions must separate speed metrics from risk quality. Any valuer consistently faster than the system average should be reviewed, not blindly rewarded.
2. Ask one mandatory question in every report: "Who is the likely buyer of this property in a forced sale scenario?" If the answer is unclear, the asset is risky, regardless of paperwork.
3. Sympathy must never replace market reality. Affordable housing does not mean affordable risk. A valuer must consciously separate borrower intent from asset exitability.
4. Valuer incentives must be delinked from disbursements. Any system that indirectly rewards conversion over caution will eventually create salesmen, not valuers.

CHAPTER 14

The Problem of OTC Conditions in Valuations

In my experience of valuing more than 1 lakh affordable customers, my biggest takeaway is that most fraud does not originate from forged documents or clever borrowers. They originate from ***OTC conditions*** that were identified, marked, but never closed, often by the same departments that flagged them.

The intent is rarely malicious. It is operational. Files are moved to meet targets; loans are booked to meet numbers, and OTCs are treated as future problems. Valuation becomes a step in the booking process, not a gatekeeper. This chapter is not about what went wrong on paper. It is about what we all saw and chose not to follow through.

OTC conditions rarely arrive as instructions. They arrive as context.

- "This is a priority case."
- "Customer is taking a loan from somewhere else, and there are no such conditions marked."
- "Branch is under business stress."
- "Try to see if this works."

Nothing unethical is said. Nothing illegal is demanded. But the frame is set. The valuation is no longer about what the asset is. It quietly becomes about what the loan needs to be. OTC conditions don't ask for false values; they ask for flexible interpretation.

Generally, many common conditions are marked to be checked by the respective departments before the handover of the final cheque, and each department marks its own set of conditions, which then go to the operations team for final check to handover the cheque to the customer or execute the final disbursement.

Conditions such as:

- Identification documents, if something is lacking at the property site.
- Disbursement to be done once 100% construction is complete at the site.
- The electricity bill is to be collected before the handover of the final cheque.
- Property tax to be collected before handover.
- ***Neighbor check*** to be done jointly before the handover of the cheque.

Let us understand from an example:

A modest house, a small loan. The valuer started his day late but carried out five site visits in four different areas. He was running out of time already and had to rush to complete all the pending visits.

He visited his first customer and started doing the exercise as required for valuation. Took out his measuring tape and measured the site. It was a 25×30 sq yd plot on paper; however, the dimensions at the site looked different. He avoided and moved on to check the identification proof.

The electricity bill was requested, but the customer replied, "Sir, woh toh nahi rakhte hamesha sath." (Sir, I don't always have it with me.)

When it came to property tax, the borrower produced an old receipt, not the latest one. He said that the new receipt was with the municipal office and would be collected soon.

"Waise bhi tax toh barta hi hoon," he added. (I file the tax anyway.)

The valuer had written all the facts on the paper and moved on to his next visit.

A neighbor check would have been required, but since he was in a rush that day, he avoided this part of the due diligence.

The valuer completed the checklist and came back to the office in the evening. The report had to be submitted, so he started preparing it.

Nothing in the report was false. Nothing was forged. Nothing was deliberately hidden, but still, everything depended on his decision.

He released all the reports with the following conditions marked as "OTC".

- Identification documents, if something is lacking at the property site.
- Disbursement to be done once 100% construction is complete at the site.
- The electricity bill is to be collected before the handover of the final cheque.
- Property tax to be collected before handover.
- Neighbor check to be done jointly before the handover of the cheque.

Each adjustment felt small. Together, they shaped the risk.

Months later, when the borrower defaulted, and recovery visited the same house, the questions returned. Louder, sharper, unanswered.

The neighbors had opinions now. The electricity connection had no ownership. Property tax was forged. And no one remembered whether those conditions had been verified or not.

Lesson 14#

In valuation, the greatest risk is often not what was missed, but what was identified and left unresolved. Conditions noted but not closed become tomorrow's losses.

Recommendations from the chapter

1. No single OTC condition should stand alone. OTC in housing finance is a misused tool. Most of us know about it, but still cannot help it. It should be managed strictly, and eradicating such conditions should be the responsibility of the risk teams.
2. Neighbor check cannot be assumed. "Not Available" is not clearance. If a neighbor is skipped, it must be explicitly stated, not converted into an OTC condition. If it is a part of the upfront checklist, it must be produced unless there is no neighbor available.
3. Institutions should promote the culture of OTC-less lending.In the era of growing assets under management, we forget to maintain quality. If anything is meant to be changed, the change should come from the system.

CHAPTER 15

When Right Decision Has No Rulebook

The case that refused to fit into the valuation theory.

It was a small house on the edge of a growing town—technically eligible, legally compliant, and mathematically safe. The land was converted. The documents were clean. LTVs were fitting well. On paper, it was a clean case.

But on ground, it was a completely different story. The property was part of a family campus, cutting across multiple houses owned by relatives. There was a common gate to enter. And then started a narrow shared passage. The ***approach road*** existed, but only if the other relatives allowed it. The house stood solid, but the drainage line passed inches from its foundation.

The borrower spoke confidently but avoided questions around local arrangements.

I asked him a simple question, "Yeh road kiski hai?" (Whose road is this?)

He smiled. "Sab use karte hain." (Everyone uses it.)

That answer sounds harmless to an untrained ear. But every valuer knows that shared use is not legal access.

There was no written denial. No dispute. No obstruction. Just borrowed convenience.

The books would call this "approach road available". But will we be able to sell this property in an open auction? That question doesn't appear in any checklist. Yet, it decides everything.

I did not reject the case. I did not approve it either. I marked it unfit for mortgage lending. Not because it violated rules but because it violated predictability.

The branch was confused.

"But Sir, sab toh theek hai..." (But, Sir, everything is okay.)

"Yes," I said. "Today."

No one argued. But no one celebrated either. Because practical decisions rarely get applause. They get acceptance or silent resistance.

Lesson 15#

Not every acceptable case on paper is a safe case on ground. When policy is silent, professional judgement becomes the real rulebook.

Recommendations from the chapter

1. Prioritize exit behavior over entry compliance. Ask yourself one practical question: "Will we be able to liquidate this asset in distress?" If the answer is no, the decision is already made.
2. Remember: Policy protects systems. Judgment protects outcomes. A valuer's role is not limited to rule adherence; it extends to foresight.
3. Accept that practical decisions are harder to defend. Decisions based on judgment often face internal resistance. Resistance does not make them wrong.
4. Learn the art of saying NO. The hardest step for any valuer is not technical; it is psychological. Saying no today protects you tomorrow.
5. The reverse is also possible; recognize it. Sometimes, documents may not fully align, yet the asset is clearly marketable. Practical judgment should work both ways, not just for rejection, but also for acceptance.

CHAPTER 16

Valuation — Not a Support Function

In most housing finance institutions, valuation reports sometimes to Credit, sometimes to Risk, and sometimes to Operations. That, by itself, is not the problem. The problem begins when reporting is confused with alignment.

Valuation may report into Credit for efficiency; it may sit under Risk for governance; it may be placed where workflows make sense. But valuation must never be expected to think like the function it reports to.

- Credit optimizes approval.
- Risk optimizes capital protection.
- Valuation must optimize the truth about the asset.

That truth should not bend based on who signs the appraisal form.

When valuation reports to Credit, it starts hearing:

- "This borrower is strong."
- "Cashflows are comfortable."

- "Structure will mitigate this."

When valuation reports to Risk, it starts hearing:

- "We need defensible logic."
- "Keep us aligned with policy."
- "Avoid being an outlier."

None of this is wrong, but the danger is subtle. Valuation slowly begins to inherit the lens of its parent function. That is when independence erodes, but through proximity.

Independence is not about where valuation sits; it is about where valuation is allowed to speak without consequence.

Can a valuer say:

- "This asset does not suit for institutional lending."
- "***Exit risk*** is disproportionate to downsize."
- "Value may be defendable, but liquidity is weak."

The housing finance ecosystem operates on momentum. Disbursement creates confidence. Confidence creates targets. Targets create pressure.

Valuation must be the one function that does not absorb momentum.

It must be allowed to feel isolated. Uncomfortable, and occasionally unpopular. That loneliness is not dysfunction; it is design.

Credit needs valuation to challenge optimism. Risk needs valuation to challenge compliance comfort. If valuation agrees too easily with either, it stops adding value.

Lesson 16#

Valuation may sit within an organization, but it must never think like the department it reports to. Its duty is not approval or policy comfort; it is to share the objective truth about the asset.

Recommendations from the chapter

1. Separate reporting from intellectual alignment. Valuation may report to Credit, Risk, or Operations for workflow efficiency. However, its analytical independence must remain non-negotiable. Reporting lines must not shape conclusions.
2. Formalize the right to disagree. Create structured documentation where valuation can record dissenting views without dilution. A disagreement vote must be treated as risk intelligence, not obstruction.
3. Protect the language of realism. Institutionalize acceptance of statements related to ***realizability***.
4. Remove volume-based metrics from valuation KPI's. Valuation must not be assessed on conversion ratios, approval speed, or disbursement alignment. Measure it by portfolio quality, reduction in exceptions, and downside containment.
5. Include valuation in strategic expansion decisions. New geographies, new builder tie-ups, or revised LTV bands must involve valuation input before launch, not after stress emerges.

PART: 2

CHAPTER 17

The Psychology of Property Buyers

In valuation, it is easy to believe that property prices move only because of economics. Market demand rises, supply tightens, interest rates fluctuate, and values adjust accordingly. These explanations appear rational and are often supported by data and reports.

But anyone who has spent enough time observing property markets closely knows that something deeper influences how real estate behaves.

Property markets are not only economic systems. They are psychological systems.

Behind every transaction lies a human decision—a buyer choosing a neighborhood, a family deciding where they want to live, or an investor believing that a particular area will grow in the future. These decisions are rarely based only on numbers.

They are shaped by perception, aspiration, and sometimes even emotion. For valuers and professionals working in housing finance, understanding the psychology of property buyers becomes an essential skill. Because the true market value of a property is ultimately determined not by its construction cost or land area, but by what buyers believe it is worth. And belief, in real estate, is a powerful force.

For most families in India, buying a house is not just a financial transaction. It is a milestone.

Owning a home represents stability, achievement, and security. It often reflects years of savings, sacrifices, and long-term planning. Many families see the purchase of a home as one of the most important decisions of their lives. This emotional dimension significantly shapes buyer behavior.

A buyer may stretch beyond their comfortable budget if the property "feels right". A family may reject technically superior houses simply because the neighborhood does not match their expectations. In many cases, the final decision is influenced by how the property makes the buyer imagine their future life. Valuers observing the market quickly realize that people do not buy houses the way institutions evaluate them.

Institutions evaluate risk. Buyers evaluate dreams.

And the intersection of those two perspectives is where the real property market operates.

The Power of Neighborhood Perception

One of the strongest psychological drivers in real estate is the perception of a neighborhood.

Two streets separated by only a few hundred meters can have dramatically different market behavior. One may attract buyers easily, while the other struggles to generate interest. Often, the difference cannot be explained entirely through infrastructure or documentation. Instead, it lies in reputation.

Neighborhood reputation builds slowly. It emerges through word of mouth, social perception, and collective experiences of residents. If a locality is seen as safe, well-connected, and socially stable, buyers gain confidence in purchasing property there.

Once confidence appears, demand begins to follow. This demand gradually strengthens property values, creating a cycle where reputation reinforces price.

Valuers often detect these shifts before formal data captures them. They hear local brokers discussing which areas buyers prefer. They notice where new families are moving. They observe where construction activity is increasing. These signals reflect the psychology of the market. The market moves when buyers begin to believe in a place.

Fear and Confidence in Property Decisions

Property markets are also strongly influenced by cycles of fear and confidence. When buyers feel confident about economic stability, employment prospects, and infrastructure development, they are more willing to commit to property purchases. Demand increases, transactions rise, and market activity becomes visible.

But when uncertainty appears, buyer psychology shifts quickly. Potential buyers delay decisions. Investors wait for clearer signals. Transactions slow down even if prices remain stable on paper.

For valuers and housing finance institutions, these psychological cycles often explain why markets behave unpredictably despite stable economic indicators.

Real estate is not a stock market where prices adjust instantly. It is a market where human sentiment quietly shapes demand over time.

The Influence of Social Signals

Property buyers rarely act in isolation. They are influenced by the decisions of others.

If many families begin moving into a particular locality, new buyers perceive that the area must offer advantages. If construction activity increases, it signals confidence in the neighborhood's future. Even small social signals—such as the opening of a new school, grocery store, or clinic—can reinforce buyer confidence. These signals create what might be called collective psychology.

Once enough people believe that a locality will grow, the belief itself begins to drive growth.

The phenomenon can be observed in many expanding cities. Areas that once seemed peripheral suddenly become attractive once a few early buyers establish the neighborhood. Over time, infrastructure improves, financial institutions begin lending there, and the market stabilizes.

From the outside, it appears as if development followed infrastructure. Development often followed belief.

Another psychological factor that shapes property decisions is familiarity.

Buyers often prefer neighborhoods that feel socially comfortable. Proximity to family, community networks, workplaces, and cultural environments play a significant role in property selection. Even when more affordable or technically superior options exist elsewhere, buyers may avoid unfamiliar locations.

For lenders and valuers, this explains why certain markets remain consistently liquid while others struggle to attract attention.

Liquidity is not determined only by infrastructure. It is also determined by how comfortable buyers feel about living there.

Aspirations and the Idea of Progress

Real estate is deeply connected to aspiration.

When buyers select a property, they are not only evaluating the present condition of the house. They are imagining the future of the neighborhood. They ask themselves questions about how the area might evolve:

- Will better roads come here?
- Will schools and markets develop nearby?
- Will the value of the property increase over time?

These expectations influence buyer willingness to pay.

Sometimes buyers purchase property in developing areas because they believe that the locality will improve significantly in the future. In other cases, they prefer established neighborhoods because they value stability over speculation. Both decisions are driven by how buyers imagine progress.

For valuers, observing these expectations becomes an important part of understanding market dynamics.

Why Some Houses Never Sell

Psychology also explains why some properties struggle to attract buyers despite reasonable valuations.

In many cases, there may be nothing technically wrong with the property. The construction may be sound, documentation may be acceptable, and the location may appear adequate on paper. Yet buyers hesitate.

The reason may lie in subtle psychological signals—a narrow access lane, an isolated street, a neighborhood perceived as stagnant, or simply a lack of activity in the surrounding market. Buyers prefer places where they see evidence of life.

Empty streets and inactive neighborhoods create doubt, even if the property itself is perfectly functional. This is why marketability cannot be explained by price alone. It is also shaped by how buyers feel about the environment surrounding the property.

Understanding buyer psychology helps valuers interpret markets more accurately. It reminds professionals that valuation is not only about calculating numbers. It is about understanding how people perceive places. A valuer who observes buyer behavior carefully can often predict which areas will become more active in the future and which markets may remain stagnant.

The technical aspects of valuation remain important—measurement, construction quality, and comparable transactions all provide necessary data. But these elements alone cannot explain the full picture.

The psychology of buyers fills the gap between numbers and reality.

The Human Side of the Market

Perhaps the most fascinating aspect of property markets is that they are ultimately built on human decisions.

Each house that is purchased represents a family making a long-term commitment to a place. Each neighborhood that grows reflects collective choices made by hundreds of such families.

When viewed from this perspective, valuation becomes more than a technical profession. It becomes a way of observing how people choose to build their lives. And the more closely one watches these choices unfold across streets and neighborhoods, the clearer it becomes that the true drivers of property markets are not just interest rates or infrastructure plans. They are the hopes, fears, and expectations of the people who decide which place they want to call home.

CHAPTER 18

Balance Transfer — The Illusion of Safety

On the surface, nothing feels risky. In fact, it feels like low-effort growth. But balance transfer (BT) is one of the misunderstood products in housing finance, because it carries borrower stability with embedded market timing risk. I will try to put my experience into writing through different angles.

Borrower's Angle

From the borrower's perspective, the balance transfer is rational. Negotiated interest rates, higher eligibility, top-up funding, and better service, but borrower motivation sometimes hides context.

- Are they rate shopping?
- Are they refinancing at a market peak?
- Are they extracting equity because resale liquidity has slowed?
- Are they migrating from a lender tightening exposure or service issues?

Borrowers rarely transfer randomly; they move when incentives shift.

The Competitive Angle

For lenders, BT cases are seductive. Why?

- Acquisition cost is lower than fresh sourcing.
- Early delinquency probability is statistically lower.
- Portfolio seasoning improves headline metrics.

BT growth improves optics, but competition creates pressure. If one lender relaxes LTV for BT cases, others follow. If one lender approves top-up aggressively, the market standard adjusts. Balance transfer can quietly become a competitive escalation tool, and competitive escalation often ignores collateral depth.

The Valuation Angle

This is where subtlety matters most. Fresh cases start from doubt; BT cases start from assumption.

It has already been valued. It has already been funded. It has already survived.

But valuation should ask a different question: "What was true then that may not be true now?"

Over time, markets change as new supply enters, employment patterns shift, access conditions evolve, and civic risks emerge or intensify.

Three years of repayment history does not validate three years of market resilience. Valuation must treat BT as a new underwriting event, not a continuation.

The Liquidity Angle

This is the most underestimated dimension. BT often happens during later-stage optimism.

Borrowers refinance when: Property value appears strong. The LTV cushion looks attractive. Equity extraction feels safe. But late-stage optimism precedes a plateau.

When liquidity slows, borrowers refinance before distress appears, not because they are weak, but because they sense market saturation.

The Portfolio Angle

Individually, BT cases look stable, but collectively, they may cluster. A branch aggressively acquiring BT in one micro-market may unknowingly accumulate exposure at peak cycle valuation because BT files often originate from the same growth phase.

If many assets were funded during the same optimistic period and transferred during the early slowdown, portfolio risk synchronizes.

Correlation enters quietly. BT may look like diversification by lender, but it is not diversification by geography or timing.

The Top-Up Temptation

Top-up is where BT risk multiplies. Strong repayment history justifies additional exposure, but equity extraction should depend on current exit feasibility, not historical price appreciation. An asset may have been appreciated on paper, but if buyer absorption has weakened, incremental exposure increases the severity of the risk. Top-up without liquidity reassessment is leverage layered over optimism.

The Psychological Angle

The biggest risk in BT is familiarity bias, and the case feels safe. The borrower feels disciplined. The documentation feels seasoned. And when things feel safe, scrutiny relaxes subtly. Valuation comments are often shortened or ignored, and this is when underwriting shifts from investigation to validation.

I have seen many late-night month-end calls depend on this psychological angle.

"BT case hai. Kar do, customer kahin nai jaega." (It's a BT case. Do it. The customer won't go anywhere.)

But post the seasoning of the portfolio, these calls haunt everyone with regret.

Recommendations from the chapter

1. Treat BT cases as fresh underwriting. Valuation should not hide behind product type. Valuers should reassess liquidity, market depth, and exit feasibility independently of previous funding and shrug pressure off their

shoulders of a decision already made by another Bank/HFC. Opinion should be irrespective of the factors of the product.

2. Recalculate LTV based on the current value and not on the historical value. I have witnessed many leaders expect the valuation of BT cases to be exactly the same or more, irrespective of accumulating the data related to micro-market evolution and current trends, and ponder highly on giving the exact value what's been given by other financial institutions. Valuers need to understand that every HFC has its own style of embracing the risk, and the valuation should be independent of all such factors. It is advised to calculate LTV on current market trends based on the recent transactions and not rely on any archaic valuation.
3. Review the BT portfolio in the risk management committees. In this era of digitization, there are enough tools to review the behavior of the products. Use of modern-day technologies to onboard customers is always welcomed by managements, but allocating budget for risk for using such tools, that's what differentiates an organization from becoming stable in the long term.

Most of us are part of this ecosystem and may have shied away from presenting the abnormalities in board/committee meetings, but if we promote such a culture in the organization where showing these signals is okay, then we can call ourselves an institutional builder, and not just an employee for some organization.

CHAPTER 19

The Ecosystem Nobody Mentions in the Sanction Letter

The Indian mortgage ecosystem is a fascinating theatre. On paper, it looks structured- ECL models, Capital adequacy ratios, RBI circulars, municipal approvals, Gram Panchayat *NOCs*, geo-tagged inspections. But on ground, it is a choreography between the daily-wage mason, the local broker who knows which patwari to call, the municipal corporation clerk who says, "file dekh lenge," (We'll see the file), the builder promising drainage, "next month pakka," (Next month definitely), and the lender trying to calculate ROA in Excel.

Capital enters the village with confidence, but the village operates on reputation. A borrower may show clean bureau history and informal salary credits, but his property might sit on a deep lane that exists only because the Gram Panchayat hasn't objected yet. A municipal corporation may have approved a layout, but the water supply is still through tanker politics. In affordable housing, formal finance rests on semi-formal land, informal access, and very formal optimism.

Competition in the ecosystem is not abstract. It is hyperlocal. Competition is massive, three lenders operating in the same ward, chasing the same G+1 semi-furnished house. One stretches the LTV to 80%, and the others match it. One promises the best-in-class rate of interest, and the others match it. Local brokers circulate the LTV and rate sheets like restaurant menus.

Builders quietly say, "Sir, funding ho jayega," (Sir, funding will be managed), and somewhere between a sanction letter and a site visit, philosophy begins negotiating with pressure.

The ecosystem rewards speed, not reflection. Growth decks speak of penetration levels and under-mortgaged India, but no slide captures the fragility of an access road that becomes a river during the monsoon.

Private capital adds another rhythm. PE wants scale. The debt market wants stability. The public market wants quarterly predictability. The branch wants targets. The borrower wants possession before Diwali. The municipal officer wants compliance, or at least documentation that looks like compliance. Everyone is rational in isolation. Collectively, the pressure accumulates, and valuation becomes the quiet negotiator in the middle- expected to be prudent but not obstructive, cautious but not slow, independent but not inconvenient.

The real truth of Indian mortgages is this: the ecosystem is neither chaotic nor perfectly structured. It is adaptive. It stretches when capital is abundant and tightens when liquidity fades. A village that looks disciplined today can feel saturated tomorrow. An MC zone with rising prices can freeze if infrastructure delays extend, and yet, sanction letters continue to print, the comparable continues to align, and the dashboards continue to grow.

The ecosystem doesn't fail loudly; it adjusts silently. The gram panchayat boundaries shift, informal layouts regularize, borrowers prepay when they can and negotiate when they must. The mortgage industry calls this resilience. Sometimes it is, sometimes it's just momentum.

If you step back long enough, you realize something quietly amusing. We speak of underwriting models, IRR, capital efficiency, and portfolio seasoning, but much of the system depends on whether the local broker can find a buyer within 90 days of possession. Behind every Excel sheet sits a street, and on that street sits an iron gate, and behind that gate sits a family whose home is both an emotional asset and a financial instrument. The ecosystem is not built in conference rooms. It was built in lanes where the drainage may or may not connect to the municipal line yet.

And that is the Indian mortgage reality; formal capital navigating informal foundations, quarter-on-quarter growth meeting monsoon season, ROE calculations resting on gram panchayat. It is complex, resilient, occasionally optimistic but always human.

The real question is not whether the ecosystem will change. It always does. The real question is whether institutions inside it are shaping their standards, or simply adjusting to its pressure.

CHAPTER 20

When Collateral Went Digital — But the Map Is Still Catching Up

India has digitized almost everything. You can verify identity through Aadhaar, pay through UPI, open a bank account with e-KYC, and even sign a document digitally while sitting in a tea shop. The mortgage industry has followed the same direction. Today, a lender can download land records from a government portal, pull property tax details from a municipal corporation website, geo-tag a site visit, and attach satellite images to a valuation report. The collateral file that once lived in a steel cupboard has slowly moved into a digital server.

But land, unlike identity or banking, carries history. And history is not easy to digitize.

Across many states, governments have worked to digitize cadastral maps—the detailed maps that define survey numbers and land parcels. These maps are the backbone of any formal land record system. In theory, once cadastral maps are digitized and superimposed on satellite imagery, every parcel of land should become clearly identifiable. A lender should be able to zoom into a map, locate the exact plot, verify its survey number, and confirm its boundaries.

In practice, things are rarely that simple. In many towns and peri-urban belts, affordable housing colonies did not grow through carefully plotted cadastral planning. They grew through gradual subdivision. A farmer sells part of his land. A small layout emerges. Another road gets cut through later. Houses come up before municipal boundaries expand. The cadastral map may still show the original agricultural parcel, while the satellite image clearly reveals dozens of houses standing on it.

When officials attempt to superimpose the cadastral map over the satellite layer, the lines do not always match perfectly. A road may appear where the map shows farmland. A cluster of houses may exist where the cadastral record still reflects one large survey plot. Digitization exposes the mismatch between the legal map and the lived map.

Mortgage institutions operate right inside this gap.

Valuers today routinely attach geo-tagged photographs to their reports. The property location is recorded with coordinates. The satellite image is marked. The lender can visually confirm that a house exists at that location. Technology provides clarity that did not exist earlier.

The geo-tag only proves location; the cadastral map proves legal identity. And sometimes those two layers are still learning how to agree with each other.

Affordable housing settlements particularly reveal this tension. Many such colonies originate in gram panchayat jurisdictions where planning regulations are lighter, and layouts evolve organically. Over time, as cities expand, these areas get absorbed into municipal limits. The houses are real, electricity connections exist, property taxes may even be paid locally, yet the cadastral update process takes time.

None of this necessarily means the asset is illegitimate. It simply reflects how Indian cities expand faster than administrative records can be updated.

This is why site visits remain important even in a digitized environment. A digital map can show the parcel. The geo-tag confirms the coordinates. But only a physical inspection reveals whether the surrounding neighborhood has stabilized, whether access roads are functional, and whether the settlement has matured into a viable residential ecosystem.

Digitization has therefore improved the visibility of collateral dramatically. It has made records easier to verify, reduced documentation friction, and introduced technological tools like geo-tagging and satellite overlays into the mortgage process.

But digitization is still reconciling two different maps of India. One map lives in cadastral records, drawn through decades of administrative surveys. The other lives on satellite images, showing how towns and villages have actually grown. The mortgage ecosystem sits right where those maps meet.

And as cadastral records, satellite imagery, and geo-tagged verification slowly converge, collateral in India will become clearer, more transparent, and easier to finance. Until then, lenders, valuers, and borrowers will continue navigating that fascinating overlap, where the cadastral boundary meets the real street, and the digital map slowly learns the geography of everyday life.

CHAPTER 21

What Valuation Really Teaches You About India

At first glance, valuation looks like a profession built on numbers. There are formats to follow, measurements to verify, comparables to study, and a final figure to conclude. A valuation report appears neat and structured—a summary of market value, supported by photographs, coordinates, and observations.

But anyone who has spent enough years in this profession eventually realizes something unexpected.

Valuation is not really about property. It is about understanding India.

Because the moment you step out of the office and begin walking through the streets where the collateral actually exists, the country begins to reveal itself in ways that no spreadsheet ever could.

A valuation assignment may begin with a survey number and an address, but by the time the site visit ends, you have witnessed something far larger—the way a neighborhood grows, the way families build their lives around a home, and the way an entire ecosystem quietly supports the value of a single house.

Over time, valuers become accidental observers of India's transformation.

If you look at a city from the perspective of an urban planning map, everything appears organized. Roads are straight lines, sectors are clearly defined, and residential zones follow neat grids. But a valuer knows that the real story of Indian cities is written differently.

Cities in India rarely grow exactly as planned. They grow from the street outward. A village becomes a cluster of houses. A cluster becomes a colony. A colony slowly attracts shops, schools, and transport. And one day, a bank arrives and begins financing homes there.

By the time a planning authority officially recognizes the neighborhood, life has already moved in. Valuers witness this transformation repeatedly. A place that was once farmland becomes a residential street. A dusty road begins to carry school buses and grocery deliveries. A few houses appear first, then dozens more follow.

The market moves first. Documentation follows later. And somewhere between those two realities sits the valuation report, trying to interpret a market that is always slightly ahead of the system designed to regulate it.

India is a country where two systems often exist side by side. There is the formal system—the one built on regulations, land records, cadastral maps, and municipal approvals. And then there is the system that operates on the ground—where people build houses slowly, sometimes room by room, where colonies evolve before authorities update their maps, and where a road can become important simply because enough people start using it.

Valuers learn to navigate both worlds.

They read land records and legal documents carefully. But they also observe the street outside the property—the movement of people, the presence of shops, the rhythm of daily life.

Because sometimes the paperwork looks perfect, but the neighborhood has no real market, and sometimes the paperwork is incomplete, but the street is full of activity and demand. Understanding this balance between formal records and lived reality is one of the most important lessons valuations teaches. One of the most fascinating discoveries in housing finance is that mortgage repayments are not driven by abstract economic models. They are driven by the small economies of everyday life.

A house may be financed through a formal loan agreement, but the EMI is often paid through income that comes from very real, very local sources:

- A shopkeeper selling groceries in the corner store.
- A contractor managing small construction projects.
- A driver navigating the city's expanding roads.
- A teacher running evening tuition classes for neighborhood children.

These small economic activities create the cash flows that support mortgages across the country.

Valuers observe this reality constantly. When they visit a property, they notice the small businesses nearby, the local markets, the workshops, and service providers that sustain the neighborhood. Behind every house stands a micro-economy. And behind every mortgage stands a family working quietly to protect that home.

Banks speak the language of collateral. The property becomes a security against the loan. It is measured, documented, and assigned a value.

But for the family living inside the house, the property means something entirely different. It is not just collateral; it is stability. It is the place where children grow up. It is the address relatives recognize. It is the symbol that the family has finally secured its own place in the world. Valuers see this emotional dimension up close. When they inspect a house, they are often greeted by homeowners who proudly explain how they built it—sometimes over many years, sometimes with savings accumulated through enormous effort.

Behind the walls and the floor tiles lies a story of patience. A valuation report cannot capture that story fully. Yet every experienced valuer senses it. And that understanding subtly influences how one begins to think about property markets. Because real estate in India is not only a financial asset. It is also a social milestone.

Technology is rapidly transforming the mortgage ecosystem. Digital land records, GIS mapping, geo-tagged inspections, and systems like DIGIPIN are making property identification more precise. Automated valuation models are beginning to analyze transaction data across entire regions.

These developments will undoubtedly make valuation more efficient, but there is a limit to what data alone can explain. A digital map can show a parcel boundary. A transaction database can reveal past sale prices. An algorithm can generate a statistical estimate of value. But none of these systems can fully capture the subtle signals that experienced valuers notice instantly.

The way buyers feel about a particular street. The reputation of a neighborhood. The quiet confidence that a new road has brought to a once-forgotten locality. These signals live in the human perception of a place. And they are often the difference between a house that sells quickly and one that waits quietly on the market.

Perhaps the greatest lesson valuation teaches is humility.

The longer one works in the field, the more one realizes that no model, no policy, and no system can fully capture the complexity of a country as diverse as India.

Markets behave differently in every region. Neighborhoods evolve in unexpected ways. Borrowers show resilience that spreadsheets rarely predict. The profession slowly transforms the valuer into something unexpected, a student of the country itself.

Each inspection becomes a small lesson about how India functions. Each street reveals something about the aspirations of the people who live there. Each house represents a step in the long journey of families seeking stability and progress.

Valuation may begin with square feet and market comparables. But it ends with a deeper understanding of how a nation grows.

After years in the profession, one realization quietly settles in. The job was never only about estimating property values. It was about observing a country that is constantly building itself—one house, one street, and one neighborhood at a time. And perhaps that is the most fascinating part of valuation. Because in the end, every valuation report may contain just a number. But behind that number lies a story about India itself. And the street always knows the truth about value.

CHAPTER 22

The Street Is the Final Teacher

Every profession eventually discovers where its real lessons come from. In valuation, the early lessons come from classrooms, guidelines, and structured reports. Young professionals learn the methods: cost approach, comparable sales, replacement values, documentation checks, and inspection procedures. The profession appears technical and orderly. Numbers are calculated carefully, formats are followed, and conclusions are written with precision.

But the moment a valuer begins walking through the streets where properties actually exist, something begins to change. The profession slowly transforms. Valuation stops being an exercise in measurement and becomes an exercise in observation. Every street visited, every house inspected, and every neighborhood explored begins to reveal something about how property markets truly function.

And the longer one spends in the field, the clearer it becomes that the street teaches lessons no manual ever could. Few professions interact with the geography of India as closely as valuers do.

Every day, valuers travel through expanding cities, semi-urban towns, and villages, gradually becoming neighborhoods. They walk through newly constructed colonies and older residential pockets. They observe how farmland slowly turns into plotted developments, how roads change the direction of growth, and how families patiently build homes over many years. In the process, valuers become quiet observers of India's transformation.

They see how a country grows—not through grand announcements or large policy documents, but through thousands of individual decisions made by families building homes.

Each inspection becomes a small story about aspiration.

- A house that took ten years to complete.
- A family that saved slowly to buy its first plot.
- A neighborhood that emerged because a road connected it to the city.

The valuation report may summarize the property in a few pages. But the real lesson lies outside the report. It lies in the street.

CHAPTER 23

The Quiet Role of Women in Mortgage Discipline

In most housing finance files, the borrower appears as a neatly defined profile. The application form records the name, occupation, income details, bureau score, and loan eligibility. The property valuation sits in another section, supported by documents, geo-tagged photographs, and market comparables. Everything appears structured and rational. The mortgage industry likes this clarity because it allows risk to be measured and decisions to be documented.

But behind many of these files lies a dimension that does not appear in the underwriting model. Inside the household, someone is quietly ensuring that the loan behaves exactly the way the spreadsheet expects it to.

In many Indian homes, that role is played by the woman of the house.

Housing finance professionals do not usually discuss this aspect openly because it sits outside formal analysis. Yet anyone who has spent time in branch offices, collection calls, or field visits eventually notices a pattern. The

EMI may be deducted from the borrower's bank account, but the rhythm of repayment is often managed by someone else in the family. She remembers when the EMI date is approaching. She reminds her husband when the account must maintain a sufficient balance. She adjusts small household expenses when income for the month feels uncertain. She carries the invisible responsibility of making sure the house—the family's most important asset—never becomes vulnerable.

Mortgage files do not contain a column for this contribution. Yet it exists in thousands of households.

The importance of home ownership in India makes this discipline even more meaningful. In many developed markets, a house can sometimes be treated as an investment decision—an asset that may be upgraded, sold, or replaced depending on financial convenience. In India, the emotional relationship with a house is deeper. The first owned home often represents years of saving, family aspiration, and social stability. It becomes the place where children grow up, where relatives gather during festivals, where the family feels rooted.

For the person who spends the most time maintaining that home—often the woman—the house carries a meaning beyond financial value. Protecting it becomes instinctive.

In the affordable housing segment, this instinct becomes even more visible. Many borrowers in this category do not have perfectly predictable income streams. A shopkeeper's earnings fluctuate with market cycles. A small contractor may receive payments irregularly. A daily wage worker's income depends on the availability of work during the month. These households operate with financial uncertainty more frequently than salaried professionals do.

Yet despite this uncertainty, many affordable housing portfolios show remarkable repayment discipline.

Lenders often attribute this to the emotional importance of the house or to strong community networks where default carries social consequences. Both explanations are valid. But another reason quietly supports this stability: the internal management of household finances.

In many homes, the woman monitors the flow of money in ways that formal financial models cannot capture. She knows when the school fee payment is due, when the electricity bill arrives, and when grocery spending needs to be reduced for a few weeks. She might not use the language of financial planning, but she practices it every day. When the EMI date approaches, she ensures that the family prepares for it.

Sometimes this preparation involves small adjustments that outsiders would barely notice. A planned purchase may be postponed. A family outing may wait until the following month. Savings set aside for another purpose may temporarily cover the EMI until income stabilizes. These decisions rarely appear dramatic, but they collectively maintain the repayment discipline that lenders observe in their portfolios.

Field officers occasionally witness these dynamics firsthand. During a property visit, a valuer may find the woman of the house supervising finishing work while discussing construction expenses with precision. When a credit officer calls regarding a delayed payment, the conversation that resolves the issue often happens with her. She explains when the next payment will be made or reassures the officer that funds will arrive after a particular business transaction. What becomes clear during these interactions is that she understands the mortgage more deeply than many assume.

She may know the loan tenure, the approximate outstanding balance, and the importance of maintaining the repayment schedule. She might not use terms like "amortization" or "interest rate reset", but she understands the practical meaning of the EMI in the household's life.

Another subtle factor strengthens this discipline. In many Indian households, women manage the micro-economy of daily spending. They know where unnecessary expenses accumulate and where savings can quietly be created. Grocery purchases, festival preparations, school supplies, clothing for children—these are areas where careful decisions can preserve financial stability.

Because of this constant involvement, women often become the first line of financial risk management within the household.

If income falls short in a particular month, she is usually the one who finds ways to rebalance the household budget. Jewelry might be pledged temporarily to raise funds. Informal savings groups may provide short-term liquidity. Relatives may be approached for temporary support. These responses happen quickly because protecting the house remains a priority.

Housing finance companies have gradually recognized the strength of this dynamic, even if they do not always articulate it directly. Many states offer reduced stamp duty when property is registered in a woman's name. Lenders often encourage joint ownership structures where the wife becomes a co-applicant or co-owner. These measures are sometimes described as steps toward gender inclusion or asset ownership equality.

While those goals are important, there is also a practical observation behind such policies. When women have a formal stake in the property, repayment discipline often strengthens further.

Ownership creates emotional commitment. When the property legally belongs to the woman as well, the house becomes even more central to the family's identity. In many cases, this increases the determination to protect the asset through consistent EMI payments.

It is important to acknowledge that this pattern does not apply to every household. India is diverse, and families' financial dynamics vary widely across regions, income groups, and social contexts. Some households distribute financial responsibility equally. In others, the husband manages the finances entirely. And in many modern urban families, both partners participate actively in mortgage planning and repayment.

Yet across thousands of mortgage accounts, housing finance professionals repeatedly encounter a familiar reality. The stability of repayment often rests on everyday financial discipline practiced inside the home. And that discipline frequently comes from the person who manages the household itself.

The mortgage industry tends to measure risk using data: bureau scores, income ratios, loan-to-value percentages, and delinquency trends. These metrics are essential for institutional decision-making. But they cannot capture every factor that contributes to repayment behavior.

Human motivation, emotional attachment to property, and internal family discipline play roles that spreadsheets struggle to quantify.

In India's housing ecosystem, these human factors are particularly powerful.

A house represents security for the next generation. It represents a place where children can grow up without the uncertainty of rental agreements. It represents progress achieved through years of effort. For many women who maintain the home every day, protecting that stability becomes a natural responsibility.

This quiet commitment rarely appears in formal discussions about mortgage risk.

Yet lenders benefit from it every single month.

When EMI payments arrive consistently, the system records another successful repayment cycle. The data reflects a number moving from one column to the next. But behind that number lies a routine that may include reminders, budgeting adjustments, conversations within the family, and small sacrifices that ensure the house remains safe.

These routines rarely appear in underwriting models. They exist in kitchens, living rooms, and conversations between family members.

The mortgage industry often speaks about portfolio quality, credit discipline, and borrower behavior. Those discussions are important, and they guide institutional strategies. But sometimes the most important contributors to portfolio stability operate quietly outside the financial system itself.

Inside many homes, someone is carefully ensuring that the EMI is paid on time. She may not appear in the loan agreement as the primary borrower. She may not attend the sanction meeting or sign the credit policy. Yet every month, through small acts of financial management, she protects the house that the mortgage finances. And in doing so, she quietly strengthens the entire ecosystem of housing finance.

CHAPTER 24

The Hidden National Network of Valuers in Nation Building

Across India, there exists a quiet professional network that few policymakers, regulators, or even financial leaders fully recognize. It does not operate through government departments or national infrastructure agencies. It has no centralized headquarters and no formal command structure. Yet every day, this network travels through cities, towns, and villages, observing the physical reality of land and property across the country.

This network is made up of valuers.

Thousands of valuation professionals move across the landscape of India daily, inspecting properties for banks, housing finance companies, insurance firms, courts, and financial institutions. Their assignments may appear routine—a house inspection, a plot valuation, a building assessment. But when viewed collectively, these visits form something much larger. They form a living map of India's real estate system.

In many ways, valuers are among the few professionals who consistently stand at the intersection of documentation and physical land. A valuer does not only read property records; he walks the street where the property stands. He checks the access road, observes the surrounding houses, studies the neighborhood activity, and understands how the market perceives that location.

While digital systems may show survey numbers and parcel boundaries, the valuer sees the actual life of the property. He notices whether the road exists in reality or only on a layout plan. He observes whether the surrounding houses indicate a growing neighborhood or a stagnant one. He understands whether buyers are active in the locality or whether transactions are rare.

This ground-level intelligence exists across thousands of valuation assignments every day. And yet, as a nation, we rarely think of valuers as a coordinated national asset.

A Network That Already Covers the Country

Unlike many professional ecosystems that are concentrated in large cities, the valuation profession is geographically dispersed. Housing finance institutions operate in hundreds of districts. Banks finance homes in semi-urban towns and expanding villages. Every loan secured by property requires someone to visit the site and confirm the asset.

This requirement has quietly created a nationwide presence of valuers.

From metropolitan cities to small towns, from industrial corridors to rural settlements gradually transforming into urban clusters, valuers travel constantly. They inspect residential homes, commercial shops, agricultural plots, and mixed-use developments. Over time, they accumulate detailed familiarity with local markets.

Few other professions maintain such consistent physical engagement with the geography of the country. Urban planners may focus on cities. Surveyors may work on specific mapping projects. Government land officials often operate within defined administrative boundaries.

Valuers, however, move fluidly across all these environments. They follow the growth of the housing market itself.

Observing the Transformation of India

India's urban expansion rarely follows neat, predictable patterns. Cities grow outward, absorbing nearby villages. Agricultural land slowly converts into plotted developments. Informal colonies appear long before municipal planning authorities formally recognize them. Infrastructure projects change property demand almost overnight.

Valuers witness these transformations firsthand. A valuer who visits a town regularly may see a quiet agricultural road gradually turn into a residential street. A new highway may suddenly bring commercial activity to an area that previously had little market interest. A cluster of houses may signal the early stages of a neighborhood that will eventually attract banks and housing finance institutions.

These observations rarely appear in formal reports. But they shape the professional judgment behind every valuation.

In this way, valuers develop a unique perspective on how India's real estate landscape evolves over time.

Unlike professions that rely primarily on desk-based analysis, valuation depends heavily on observation. The valuer must interpret both documentation and physical conditions. Land records may suggest certain boundaries or ownership structures, but the ground reality sometimes tells a more complex story.

A road shown on the map may not exist physically. A large parcel recorded in land records may have been subdivided informally. A house may be built in a way that affects its marketability even if the documentation appears clean.

Understanding these nuances requires repeated field experience.

Over time, valuers develop a kind of spatial intuition—an ability to read neighborhoods and interpret how properties function within them.

This intuition becomes especially valuable in housing finance, where the long-term performance of a loan often depends on the liquidity and stability of the underlying property market.

Despite their deep engagement with the country's land ecosystem, valuers remain largely invisible in national discussions about land governance and property digitization.

Governments invest heavily in programs to modernize land records, digitize cadastral maps, and create digital addressing systems. These initiatives are important steps toward building a transparent property ecosystem.

But technology alone cannot fully capture the complexity of India's land environment.

Digital maps may show parcel boundaries. Satellite imagery may reveal physical structures. Yet understanding how those structures relate to documentation, ownership patterns, and market behavior often requires human verification.

Valuers already perform this verification daily for financial institutions. Their observations could contribute significantly to improving the accuracy of digital land systems.

As India moves toward initiatives such as DIGIPIN, geospatial mapping, and integrated digital land records, the role of professionals who understand both the map and the street becomes increasingly important.

Valuers naturally occupy this bridge.

They interpret legal records while standing physically on the property. They connect financial institutions with real-world assets. They translate a living neighborhood into a value that lenders can rely upon.

If properly integrated into national land digitization efforts, this professional network could become an important contributor to building a more accurate property database.

Thousands of inspections conducted each month already generate valuable information about location coordinates, property characteristics, and neighborhood conditions.

Harnessed thoughtfully, this data could strengthen the country's evolving digital land infrastructure.

In a country as large and diverse as India, building reliable land systems requires both sophisticated technology and widespread human engagement with the landscape. The valuation profession already provides that engagement.

Quietly, without much public attention, valuers travel across districts and neighborhoods documenting the physical reality of property markets. Their work supports the mortgage system, protects financial institutions from collateral risk, and helps borrowers access housing finance.

But beyond these immediate functions, the profession also represents something larger. It represents a hidden national network—one that understands the geography of India's real estate not through abstract data alone, but through years of walking the streets where those properties stand.

And perhaps, as the country continues its journey toward a fully digital land ecosystem, this network will begin to receive the recognition it deserves.

CHAPTER 25

Why Valuers Often Make the Best Collection Officers in Housing Finance

In most housing finance companies, valuation and collections sit in different departments. One focuses on assessing collateral before the loan is disbursed; the other steps in when repayments begin to slip.

On paper, they appear to perform entirely different roles. One evaluates value, the other recovers money. But in practice, many experienced professionals in the industry quietly acknowledge something interesting. The person who understands the asset best is often the valuer. And that is why valuers, when placed in collection or recovery roles, often perform exceptionally well.

The reason lies in the way valuers see a property. Unlike many other professionals in the lending chain, valuers interact with collateral not as paperwork but as a living asset inside a neighborhood. When a valuer visits a property, the job is not limited to measuring the ***built-up area*** or confirming the address. A good valuer observes the surroundings—the width of the road, the density of houses, the local market activity, the behavior of neighbors, and the overall liquidity of the location.

Over time, valuers develop an instinct for how a property behaves in the real market. That instinct becomes extremely valuable when a loan enters collections.

When a borrower misses multiple EMIs and the account approaches recovery discussions, the institution begins asking a critical question: What is the realistic exit value of this property? In theory, the valuation report prepared at the time of sanction should answer this question. But markets change, neighborhoods evolve, and liquidity conditions shift.

A valuer who understands the micro-market can quickly assess whether the property will attract buyers, how long a sale might take, and what price range might realistically emerge in distress. A collection officer without this ground understanding may rely purely on paperwork.

Another reason valuers perform well in collections is their familiarity with local real estate ecosystems. Real estate markets are deeply local. Every neighborhood has its own informal network of brokers, small developers, contractors, and property dealers. Valuers interact with these networks regularly during their fieldwork. They know who the active brokers are, which buyers are looking for plots, which builder is quietly acquiring houses for redevelopment, and which pockets have strong resale demand. When a stressed asset needs to be resolved, this network knowledge becomes extremely powerful.

A valuer does not begin the recovery process blindly. He already understands where potential buyers might exist.

Collections in housing finance, therefore, often become less about aggressive recovery and more about facilitating liquidity—finding a realistic exit path for the property. Someone who knows the local market can shorten that process dramatically.

There is also a psychological dimension.

Borrowers facing repayment stress often feel defensive when approached by collection teams. They may expect pressure, warnings, or legal threats. But when the person engaging with them understands the property itself—its location, its construction quality, its neighborhood—the conversation shifts slightly.

The borrower realizes that the institution understands the asset beyond the loan agreement. This can create a more constructive dialogue about possible solutions: voluntary sale, refinancing, restructuring, or negotiated settlement.

Valuers are also trained to maintain a certain level of objectivity about property value. They learn early in their careers that not every house commands the price its owner expects. Market value depends on demand, access, infrastructure, and comparable transactions. When recovery discussions involve selling the property, these realities must be communicated carefully to the borrower.

A valuer is often better equipped to explain these market realities than someone who approaches the problem purely from a financial perspective.

Another advantage lies in the valuer's familiarity with documentation and legal frameworks. During valuation assignments, professionals routinely examine sale deeds, layout approvals, municipal records, and land titles. This exposure gives them a practical understanding of how property ownership structures work.

When a loan moves toward recovery, these same documents become central again—verifying title clarity, identifying co-owners, and confirming whether a property can legally be transferred.

Valuers, therefore, enter the collection process with a head start in understanding the asset's legal framework.

There is also a subtle but important cultural factor. Valuers typically spend significant time in the field. They interact with homeowners, builders, brokers, municipal officials, and sometimes entire neighborhoods while conducting inspections. This exposure develops strong communication skills rooted in ground reality rather than corporate language.

In collections, communication matters immensely. Recovering a housing loan rarely succeeds through confrontation alone. It requires negotiation, patience, and the ability to understand the borrower's situation while still protecting the institution's capital. Field-oriented professionals often handle these conversations more effectively because they are accustomed to engaging with people from diverse backgrounds.

Perhaps the most important quality valuers bring to collections is their sense of realism about liquidity. During underwriting, valuation reports estimate market value under normal conditions. But when recovery begins, the institution must think in terms of distress liquidity—the price at which a property can actually sell within a limited time frame.

Valuers understand this distinction instinctively. They know which neighborhoods absorb distressed sales quickly and which locations struggle to attract buyers. They know whether a property is likely to sell within three months or remain unsold for a year. This judgment helps institutions design practical recovery strategies instead of relying on unrealistic expectations.

Of course, not every valuer automatically becomes an excellent collection officer. The roles still require different temperaments. Collections demand persistence, negotiation skills, and emotional resilience. But when a professional combines these qualities with a deep understanding of collateral and local markets, the results can be remarkably effective.

Housing finance, after all, is not only about lending money. It is about understanding the asset that secures the loan. When that understanding travels from valuation into collections, the institution gains something valuable: the ability to manage risk not just through numbers, but through real knowledge of the property and the market around it.

And in an industry where every loan is ultimately tied to a physical piece of land and a family home, that knowledge can make all the difference between a prolonged recovery struggle and a timely resolution.

CHAPTER 26

The Civil Engineer's Natural Profession

In many ways, valuation is one of the most natural professions for civil engineers. Civil engineering teaches the science of building—how structures stand, how materials behave, how foundations support weight. Engineers understand the physical logic of buildings in a way few others do. They can read a structure the way a doctor reads a patient's condition. But when a civil engineer enters valuation, the profession expands that knowledge.

The engineer who once focused only on structures begins to understand something larger: the relationship between construction and market behavior. A building may be technically strong, but its value depends on many other factors—location, accessibility, neighborhood growth, and buyer confidence.

Valuation allows civil engineers to apply their technical knowledge while also learning the economics of real estate.

They begin to see how infrastructure changes value. A new highway can transform farmland into a residential market. A school or hospital can raise the desirability of a neighborhood. A road widening can change how buyers perceive an entire street.

Civil engineers who enter valuation, therefore, stand at a powerful intersection where engineering meets economics.

Despite its importance, valuation remains one of the least understood professions in the financial ecosystem. Banks depend on it. Housing finance companies rely on it. Courts require it in disputes. Governments need it for land acquisition and taxation. Yet relatively few young professionals consciously choose valuation as a career path.

Many civil engineers move toward construction management or project execution. Some enter infrastructure companies, others pursue corporate roles. Very few realize that valuation offers a career that connects engineering knowledge with financial systems. And this is where the profession holds enormous potential.

India is urbanizing rapidly. Cities are expanding, housing demand continues to grow, and mortgage markets are becoming more sophisticated. Every one of these developments requires professionals who understand property not just as structures, but as assets within a larger ecosystem. Valuers play that role. They translate the physical reality of buildings into financial language that institutions can rely on.

As India continues to grow, the need for skilled valuation professionals will only increase. For the profession to reach its full potential, it must attract and nurture new talent.

Civil engineers entering the field should not see valuation as a secondary career option. It is a profession that demands judgment, observation, and a deep understanding of how markets function.

CHAPTER 27

Why Valuers Rarely Become CEOs

In the financial ecosystem, every profession carries its own identity. Credit officers understand risk. Sales teams understand growth. Finance professionals understand capital structures. And valuers understand collateral—the physical assets that stand behind every housing loan.

Among these roles, valuation occupies a particularly unique position. The valuer stands at the intersection of the financial system and the real estate market. They step outside the office, walk through streets and neighborhoods, observe construction quality, analyze location dynamics, and translate these observations into a number that the institution can rely on.

Yet despite the importance of this role, one interesting pattern can be observed across the housing finance industry. Very few valuers ever become CEOs.

This is not because valuers lack intelligence or market understanding. In fact, many valuers possess an unusually deep understanding of how the housing ecosystem functions. They see the borrower's house, the surrounding neighborhood, the quality of construction, and the liquidity of the local market. They interact with brokers, builders, municipal officials, and homeowners. In many ways, they have one of the most comprehensive views of the property ecosystem.

But leadership pathways inside financial institutions often follow a different trajectory.

The Structure of Financial Institutions

Most housing finance companies are structured around three primary pillars: sales, credit, and finance.

Sales teams drive growth by sourcing borrowers and expanding the institution's footprint across new geographies. Credit teams design risk policies, evaluate borrower profiles, and approve loan applications. Finance teams manage capital adequacy, investor relations, and regulatory reporting. These three functions tend to dominate the strategic conversations inside boardrooms.

When organizations identify future leadership, they often look toward professionals who have spent years navigating these areas. Sales leaders understand how to expand portfolios. Credit leaders understand how to control risk. Finance leaders understand how to manage balance sheets and regulatory frameworks.

Valuation, by contrast, is often treated as a support function. Its purpose is to ensure that collateral is correctly assessed before a loan is approved. Once the valuation report is submitted and the loan is disbursed, the institution's attention moves to other aspects of the lending cycle. As a result, valuation professionals rarely receive exposure to the broader strategic decisions that shape the organization.

A Profession Built on Independence

Another reason valuers rarely rise to the highest leadership positions lies in the nature of the profession itself.

Valuation requires independence.

A valuer's responsibility is to provide an unbiased assessment of property value, even when that assessment may slow down a loan approval or challenge the expectations of sales teams. This independence is essential for maintaining the credibility of the institution's risk framework.

However, independence also means that valuers often operate slightly outside the main growth engine of the organization.

They are not responsible for generating business. They are not usually involved in designing loan products or negotiating funding structures. Their work focuses on protecting the institution's capital rather than expanding it.

In many organizations, leadership tracks tend to favor roles that directly influence revenue growth or capital management.

The Gap Between Ground Knowledge and Boardroom Visibility

Perhaps the most ironic aspect of this situation is that valuers often possess knowledge that could be extremely valuable at the leadership level.

Because they spend so much time in the field, valuers understand how real estate markets evolve. They see which towns are expanding, which neighborhoods are attracting buyers, and which areas suffer from weak liquidity. They notice infrastructure developments before they appear in official reports. They observe borrower behavior in ways that financial models cannot fully capture.

In many ways, valuers hold street-level intelligence about the housing ecosystem.

Yet this knowledge rarely travels upward into strategic decision-making.

Boardroom discussions often rely on portfolio statistics, market reports, and financial projections. These tools are important, but they sometimes overlook the subtle signals that professionals in the field encounter every day.

The result is a gap between those who understand the ground and those who guide the institution.

The Skills Leadership Requires

Leadership in a housing finance company demands a wide range of capabilities beyond technical expertise. A CEO must understand regulatory frameworks, manage investor expectations, oversee capital allocation, and balance growth with risk discipline. They must also navigate organizational culture, manage large teams, and communicate effectively with regulators and shareholders.

Valuers, whose careers are often centered on field inspections and asset analysis, may not always receive the exposure necessary to develop these broader leadership skills.

This does not mean they are incapable of becoming leaders. It simply means that the institutional pathways rarely place them in positions where such development occurs.

In many organizations, the journey to leadership requires rotations across multiple functions—credit policy, portfolio management, funding strategy, and business expansion. Without access to these experiences, even the most insightful valuation professionals remain confined to their specialized domain.

A Missed Opportunity

The absence of valuers in top leadership roles may represent a missed opportunity for the industry.

Housing finance ultimately depends on the quality and behavior of collateral. Every mortgage portfolio is anchored in thousands of individual properties spread across diverse markets. Understanding how those assets behave over time is crucial for managing risk and ensuring long-term stability. Valuers, through their constant interaction with the ground reality of property markets, possess insights that could enrich strategic thinking at the highest levels.

If institutions created pathways for valuation professionals to move into broader management roles—perhaps through cross-functional exposure or strategic advisory positions—they might discover that the profession holds more leadership potential than traditionally assumed.

CHAPTER 28

The New Generation and the Old Boardroom

India's mortgage ecosystem is quietly entering a generational transition. For decades, housing finance in the country was shaped by a particular kind of professional culture—one that valued experience, hierarchy, and institutional stability. Decisions moved slowly through layers of approval. Knowledge flowed downward from senior leadership to the field. Valuers, credit officers, and branch teams learned their craft gradually, often through years of observation and mentorship.

That model built many successful institutions. But the India that produced those institutions is not the same India that is shaping the mortgage market today.

A new generation of professionals has entered the industry. They are younger, more technologically comfortable, and often far more curious about how systems can be improved. Many of them grew up in a digital environment where information moves quickly, decisions are data-driven, and experimentation is encouraged. They are not intimidated by technology platforms, analytics dashboards, or automated decision systems. In fact, they often expect such tools to exist.

When these young professionals enter housing finance companies, they bring with them a different mindset. They ask questions.

- Why is a process done this way?
- Why does a valuation report follow a particular format?
- Why are decisions delayed when data already exists?
- Why are certain risk indicators ignored even when they are visible on the ground?

Sometimes these questions lead to innovation. Sometimes they create discomfort. Because in many traditional institutions, questioning long-established processes can be interpreted as challenging authority. This is where the tension between young talent and old boardrooms quietly begins.

The Energy of Young India

Young professionals entering housing finance today often possess a broader view of the ecosystem than previous generations did at the same stage of their careers. They understand how digital land records work. They are comfortable interpreting geospatial data, transaction dashboards, and portfolio analytics. They can quickly explore data patterns that might have taken weeks to analyze in earlier systems.

More importantly, they are often closer to the realities of the market.

Many young professionals spend their early careers in branch operations, credit underwriting, or valuation fieldwork. They interact directly with borrowers, brokers, and local property markets. They see how small towns expand, how gram panchayat layouts evolve into formal colonies, and how borrowers manage their financial commitments. This exposure gives them insights that can be extremely valuable for institutions.

A young analyst might notice a pattern of loan concentration in a specific locality. A field officer may detect early signs of repayment stress among certain borrower profiles. A valuation professional may observe how infrastructure development is shifting property demand in a particular district.

If these observations are heard and acted upon, they can strengthen the institution. But for that to happen, the organization must be willing to listen.

The Silent Barrier of Ego

In many financial institutions, the greatest barrier to innovation is not a lack of technology or a lack of talent. It is ego.

Boardrooms are places where reputations have been built over decades. Senior leaders carry the weight of past decisions, past successes, and past authority. They have guided institutions through growth phases, regulatory changes, and economic cycles. Naturally, they believe in the systems that helped them reach those positions.

But sometimes, that belief can harden into resistance.

When a younger professional suggests a new approach—perhaps a data-driven valuation model, a portfolio risk visualization tool, or a change in underwriting practice—the suggestion may be perceived not as an improvement but as a criticism of existing leadership.

Instead of asking, "Is this idea useful?" the reaction becomes, "Why is this person questioning our system?"

And slowly, the organization begins to silence its own talent.

Young professionals learn that asking too many questions is risky. They learn that innovation may not be rewarded if it disrupts existing hierarchies. Over time, many of them stop offering ideas altogether.

The institution then continues operating exactly as it did before, unaware that valuable insights have quietly disappeared.

The Cost of Ignoring Young Minds

This dynamic carries a real cost for the mortgage ecosystem.

Housing finance is entering a period of enormous transformation. Digital land records, geospatial mapping, automated valuation models, and advanced analytics are reshaping how collateral and credit risk can be understood. Institutions that adapt quickly will gain advantages in efficiency, risk management, and market insight.

Young professionals are often the ones most comfortable navigating these changes. They understand technology intuitively. They are willing to experiment with new tools. They are curious about how data can reveal patterns in borrower behavior and property markets.

If institutions create space for these minds to contribute, they gain access to a powerful engine of innovation. If they suppress them, they risk becoming slow and rigid in an environment that is moving faster every year.

The Difference Between Authority and Leadership

This situation raises an important question for mortgage institutions: What kind of leadership culture will guide the industry in the future?

Authority comes from position and experience. It commands respect through hierarchy. Leadership, however, requires something more subtle—the ability to listen, adapt, and encourage the growth of others.

The best leaders in housing finance understand that knowledge does not flow in only one direction. Senior professionals carry institutional wisdom, regulatory understanding, and strategic perspective. Younger professionals bring fresh observations, technological fluency, and direct exposure to changing market behavior.

When these two perspectives meet with mutual respect, the institution becomes stronger. When they clash through ego, the institution loses both.

CHAPTER 29

A Changing Mortgage Landscape

India's housing finance market is expanding rapidly. Millions of first-time homebuyers are entering the system, especially in smaller towns and semi-urban regions. Digital platforms are transforming how borrowers interact with lenders. Property markets are becoming increasingly connected through data.

This environment demands organizations that can adapt quickly.

The institutions that thrive will likely be those that combine experience with curiosity. They will maintain the discipline and risk awareness built over decades while also encouraging younger professionals to explore new ideas.

Such organizations will treat questions not as threats but as opportunities to refine their understanding of the market.

The Future Belongs to Institutions That Listen

Young India is not waiting for permission to change industries.

Across sectors—technology, finance, logistics, and entrepreneurship—younger professionals are already reshaping how businesses operate. They build platforms faster, experiment more freely, and rely heavily on data to guide decisions. Housing finance will not remain untouched by this wave.

Institutions that recognize the value of young talent will evolve with the market. They will integrate digital tools, refine risk models, and adapt their valuation and credit frameworks to new realities. Those who remain trapped in rigid hierarchies may find themselves struggling to keep pace. Because in the end, the strength of a mortgage institution does not come only from its balance sheet. It comes from the quality of the minds inside it—and whether those minds are allowed to think freely.

The future of housing finance will not be shaped only by policies, technologies, or regulations. It will also be shaped by something far more human: "Whether the boardroom has the humility to listen to the next generation sitting just outside its doors."

CHAPTER 30

The Future of Leadership in Housing Finance

As the mortgage ecosystem evolves, the definition of leadership may also change. Digital land records, geospatial analytics, automated valuation models, and data-driven portfolio monitoring are transforming how institutions understand collateral and risk. In such an environment, professionals who combine field knowledge with analytical insight may become increasingly valuable.

Valuers already possess a deep understanding of how properties behave in the real market. If they are given opportunities to expand their exposure to credit policy, portfolio management, and financial strategy, they could become powerful contributors to institutional leadership.

Perhaps the future will see more organizations recognizing this potential.

Because the person who spends years walking through neighborhoods, observing markets, and studying the assets behind every loan may possess a perspective that boardrooms sometimes overlook. And sometimes, the best view of the mortgage industry comes not from the top floor of the office building, but from the street where the collateral stands.

CHAPTER 31

The Digital Future of Collateral — Where Valuation Is Heading

For a long time, valuation in India has been a profession rooted in physical observation. A valuer traveled to the property, measured the structure, studied the surrounding neighborhood, and compared it with recent transactions in the locality. The process relied heavily on experience, local knowledge, and professional judgment. In many ways, valuers served as the bridge between the formal financial system and the informal realities of the property market.

But the environment around them is changing rapidly.

Across India, the government has been gradually building a digital architecture for land, property, and spatial data. Initiatives such as the Digital India Land Records Modernization Programme (DILRMP) aim to bring together textual land records, cadastral maps, and property registration databases into unified digital platforms. These efforts are not merely administrative reforms; they are part of a broader vision where land and property information becomes machine-readable, interoperable, and accessible across multiple government and financial systems.

As this digital infrastructure evolves, the role of valuation will inevitably evolve with it.

The Rise of Spatial Intelligence

One of the most significant technological shifts shaping the future of collateral is the integration of geospatial data systems into land administration. Traditionally, land records existed in two separate formats: textual records that described ownership, and cadastral maps that illustrated parcel boundaries. These systems often operated independently, making it difficult to link property ownership with precise geographic coordinates.

Today, governments are working to digitize cadastral maps and superimpose them onto high-resolution satellite imagery using Geographic Information Systems (GIS). Through this process, each land parcel can be mapped with spatial accuracy, linking legal ownership data with physical land boundaries.

For the mortgage industry, this transformation could be revolutionary.

Instead of relying solely on descriptive addresses or manually interpreted maps, lenders and valuers may soon be able to identify properties through geospatial coordinates and digital parcel identifiers. This will allow institutions to visualize entire mortgage portfolios on digital maps, analyze exposure across micro-markets, and monitor geographic concentration risks in real time.

In effect, valuation will become part of a larger system of spatial financial intelligence.

DIGIPIN and the Evolution of Digital Addressing

A particularly interesting development in this direction is the emergence of DIGIPIN, a concept designed to provide every location in India with a unique digital address. Traditional addressing systems in many parts of the country rely on landmarks and local descriptions—a format that works for daily navigation but creates challenges for digital data integration.

DIGIPIN proposes a standardized location-based addressing protocol where every geographic point can be represented by a unique alphanumeric code. Unlike conventional addresses, which can vary in format or spelling, a digital pin creates a consistent identifier that can be integrated into databases, maps, and financial systems.

For valuation and mortgage lending, the implications are significant.

A property's digital address could become a permanent spatial identifier, linking the asset to multiple layers of information—cadastral boundaries, ownership records, municipal approvals, infrastructure data, and even environmental risk indicators. When a valuer visits a property, geo-tagged photographs and inspection reports could automatically be associated with the DIGIPIN location code, ensuring precise traceability.

Over time, such digital addressing systems may reduce ambiguity in property identification and improve the efficiency of property verification processes.

Automated Valuation Models and Predictive Analytics

As digital records and transaction data become more accessible, the mortgage industry is also experimenting with Automated Valuation Models (AVMs). These systems use statistical algorithms and machine learning techniques to estimate property values based on large datasets of past transactions, location characteristics, and market trends.

In mature property markets, AVMs have already become an important analytical tool. In India, their adoption is still evolving due to the diversity and fragmentation of real estate markets. Nevertheless, as data availability improves through digitized registries and spatial mapping, AVMs are expected to become increasingly useful.

Future valuation systems may combine machine learning algorithms, geospatial analytics, and transaction databases to generate preliminary property value estimates within seconds. These systems will analyze patterns such as price movements within micro-markets, infrastructure proximity, and demographic trends to provide data-driven insights.

However, even the most advanced predictive models will have limitations. Real estate markets remain influenced by factors that are difficult to quantify—neighborhood sentiment, informal community dynamics, and the subtle reputational signals that shape buyer demand. These elements are often understood best by professionals who spend time on the ground.

The future of valuation will therefore likely involve human–machine collaboration, where technology assists valuers in analyzing data while professional judgment interprets local market realities.

Blockchain, Digital Land Registries, and Title Security

Another technology that occasionally appears in discussions about land administration is blockchain-based land registries. The idea behind such systems is to create tamper-resistant digital records of property ownership that can be verified transparently across institutions.

In theory, blockchain could allow property transactions to be recorded on decentralized ledgers, reducing disputes and improving trust in land ownership records. While large-scale implementation in India is still in experimental stages, pilot projects in some regions have explored the potential for distributed ledger technology (DLT) to enhance transparency in property registration.

If such systems mature, valuation professionals may eventually operate in an environment where ownership records, transaction histories, and ***encumbrances*** are instantly verifiable through secure digital networks.

Digital Twins and the Future of Urban Valuation

Looking further ahead, another technological concept gaining attention is the idea of digital twins—virtual models of physical environments that combine spatial data, infrastructure networks, and real-time information. In urban planning contexts, digital twins can simulate how cities grow, how infrastructure affects property values, and how environmental risks may evolve over time.

For mortgage lenders, such systems could offer powerful insights. Imagine a digital platform where a property's value is influenced not only by past transactions but also by projected infrastructure developments, ***zoning*** changes, and demographic shifts.

Valuation could gradually evolve from a static assessment into a dynamic model of urban economics, continuously updated as new data flows into the system.

The Continuing Importance of Human Judgment

Despite these technological possibilities, one fundamental truth remains unchanged: property markets are deeply human ecosystems.

A digital system may identify the coordinates of a property, analyze transaction trends, and calculate statistical estimates of value. But it cannot fully capture the lived experience of a neighborhood—the way residents perceive safety, the vibrancy of local commerce, or the subtle reputation of a particular street.

These aspects continue to influence buyer behavior in ways that algorithms struggle to measure. For this reason, the valuer's role will not disappear. Instead, it will evolve.

Future valuers will likely operate as hybrid professionals, combining field observations with advanced data tools. They may interpret GIS layers, analyze automated value estimates, and verify digital land records while still walking through neighborhoods to understand the human context of the asset.

In other words, technology will change how valuers work, but it will not eliminate the need for their insight.

A Data-Driven Mortgage Ecosystem

The broader vision emerging from government initiatives and technological innovation is a mortgage ecosystem that is far more transparent, data-driven, and spatially connected than the one that exists today.

- Land records will be digitized and linked to cadastral maps.
- Properties will carry unique digital identifiers such as DIGIPIN codes.
- Valuation models will incorporate geospatial analytics and predictive algorithms.
- Mortgage portfolios will be visualized through digital mapping platforms.

Together, these developments will gradually reshape how lenders understand collateral.

Yet the core purpose of valuation will remain unchanged. At its heart, valuation will still seek to answer a simple but essential question: What is this property worth in the real market?

The difference is that in the future, the valuer will answer that question with the assistance of technologies that were unimaginable just a generation ago.

And somewhere between satellite imagery, machine learning models, and digital address systems, the profession of valuation will continue its quiet evolution—adapting to a world where property is no longer just a physical asset, but also a node in a vast digital map of land, data, and finance.

Closing Note

This book was never meant to teach valuation. It was meant to remind.

Remind that behind every report, there is a decision. Behind every decision, there is a judgment. And behind every judgment, there is a moment where we choose between what is easy and what is right.

In files, everything can be made to look complete. On ground, nothing hides for long.

Over time, I have learned that valuation does not fail in one big moment. It bends—slowly, quietly, repeatedly. Not when rules are broken. But when questions are skipped. Not when fraud happens. But when discomfort is avoided. Not when something is wrong. But when something feels wrong, and we still move ahead.

We call it process. We call it standard practice. We call it alignment. But the market calls it something else. It calls it risk. And one day, it returns.

Valuation is not a support function. It is not a checkpoint. It is not a formality in a larger process. It is the last independent voice before money meets reality. And that voice will not always be popular. It will not always be convenient. But it must always be honest.

Valuation is not about getting the number right. It is about having the courage to say when the number should not exist.

Appendix — Glossary & Acronyms

Note to the Reader

This glossary is not a textbook definition. It reflects how these terms behave in the field, not just how they are written in policy.

A. Key Terms in Valuation

Approach Road
The physical access to a property. Its existence is not enough—it must be legal, usable, and uncontested.

Built-up Area
Carpet area plus wall thickness and internal spaces.

Collateral
The property that is offered as security against a loan. Its real strength lies in its ability to be liquidated under stress.

Comparable
Recent similar property transactions used to estimate value. In informal markets, these often reflect sentiment rather than realizable value.

Disbursement
The release of loan funds to the borrower. It often creates pressure and

momentum within the system.

Encumbrance

Any legal liability or charge on a property. A clean record does not always eliminate ground-level risks.

Exit Risk

The risk associated with selling the property during recovery. A technically correct asset may still have high exit risk.

Liquidity

The ease with which a property can be sold in the market. Value without liquidity is theoretical.

Marketability

The attractiveness of a property to potential buyers, influenced by access, legality, and the surrounding ecosystem.

Micro-Market

A localized area with its own demand-supply dynamics, often behaving differently from nearby regions.

Neighbor Check

Informal verification with nearby residents regarding ownership, disputes, and property usage.

Realizability

The ability to convert a property into cash, especially under stress conditions.

Standard Practice

An informal justification used to normalize repeated exceptions.

Underwriting
The process of evaluating risk before approving a loan.

Valuation Report
A document stating the assessed value and observations of a property. Its purpose is risk signaling, not just number reporting.

Valuer
A professional who assesses property value. In practice, a valuer is a decision-maker under uncertainty.

Zoning
The classification of land (residential, commercial, agricultural). Mismatch creates legal and liquidity risks.

B. Acronyms & Their Meaning

LTV: Loan to Value
Ratio of loan amount to property value. Indicates leverage and exposure.

NOC: No Objection Certificate
A document stating no objection from a concerned authority.

OTC: Over The Counter Conditions
Conditions to be fulfilled after approval or before disbursement, often used to defer risk instead of resolving it.

RERA: Real Estate Regulatory Authority

The regulatory body governing real estate projects.

TAT: Turnaround Time

Time taken to complete a process, such as valuation or loan approval.

www.ingramcontent.com/pod-product-compliance
Lightning Source LLC
LaVergne TN
LVHW100323210926
848480LV00003B/1233
* 9 7 9 8 9 0 5 1 0 9 5 3 9 *